ANARCADIA RUTH MACLENNAN

FILM AND VIDEO UMBRELLA
JOHN HANSARD GALLERY

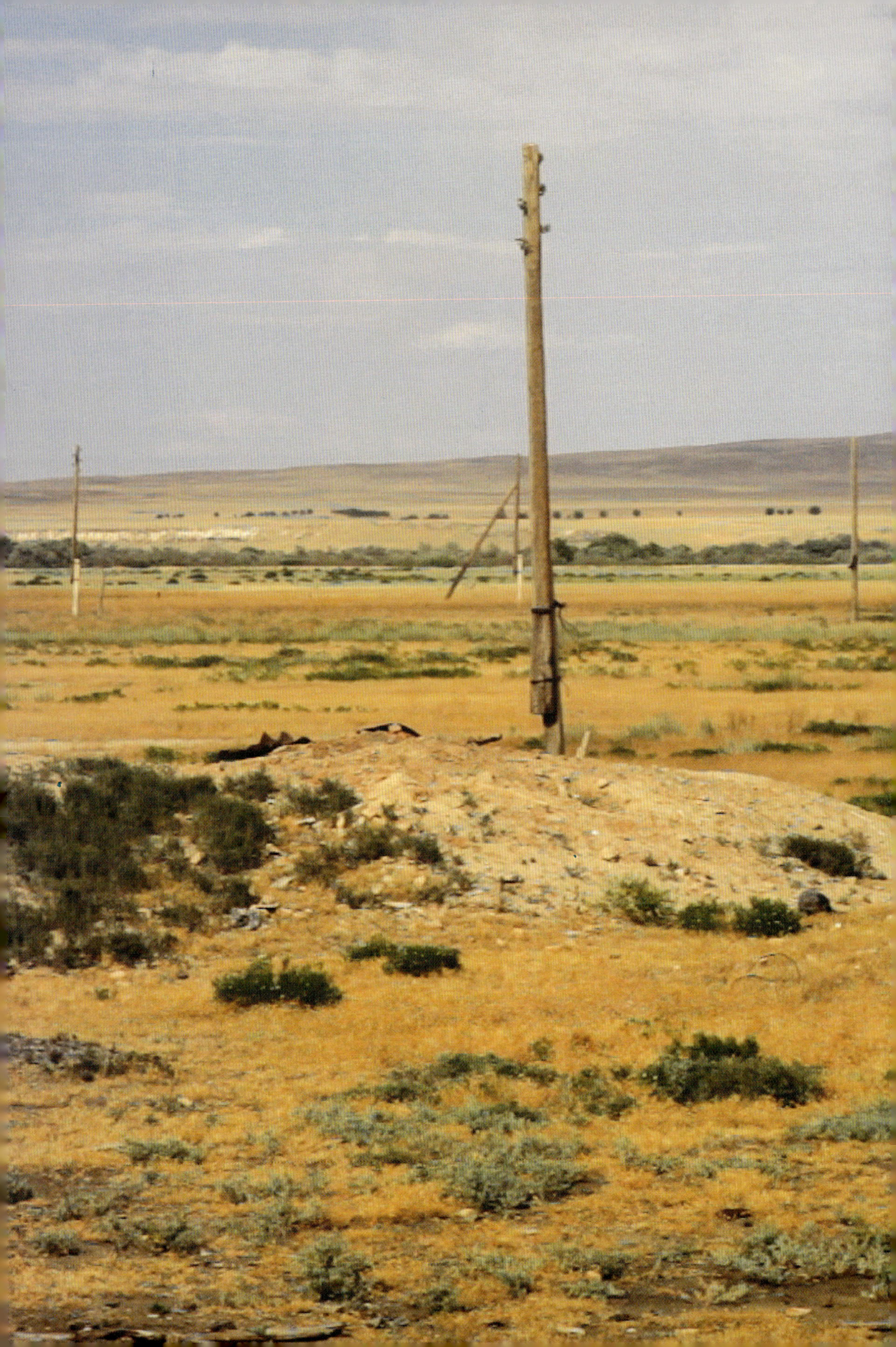

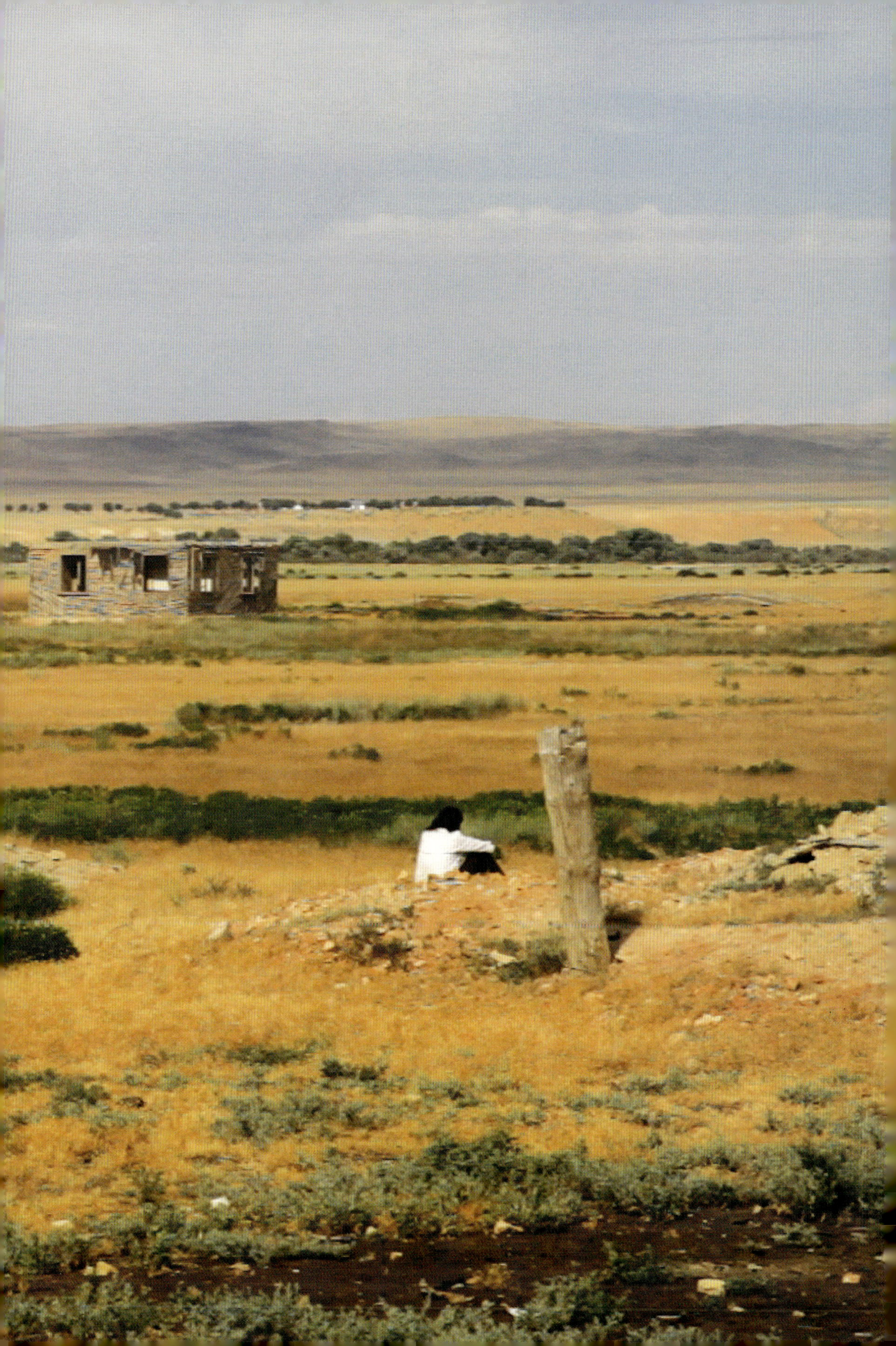

CONTENTS

ACKNOWLEDGEMENTS

This book represents five years of work and several trips to Kazakhstan. I never thought I would become hooked but I did, as have many other artists and writers before me. My journeys in this elusive and epic landscape have become an important landmark in my life and work. I am very thankful for the opportunities I have been given.

I would especially like to thank Stephen Foster and Steven Bode for their encouragement and enthusiasm, for trusting that the mirage in the desert was worth chasing, and for their acute curatorial and critical sense.

Special thanks to Bevis Bowden for his skill and inspiration on location shooting *Anarcadia* and for his critical insights during editing; to Brada Barassi for recording sound so effectively and unobtrusively; to George Drennan and Saule Suleimenova for playing their parts so beautifully; to Kuat Shildebayev for his generosity with his extraordinary music; to Mikhail Karikis for his help bringing the sound together so sensitively. Thank you to Karen Murray for production; to the British Council in Almaty; and to the Kazakhstan State Archives in Almaty for allowing me to use archive photographs and film. Thank you to Mike Jones at Film and Video Umbrella for his skill and insight installing the exhibitions of *Anarcadia*; and to Nina Ernst for her skill in editing this book. I am hugely grateful to Anna Harding, who first invited me to Kazakhstan and who with Yuliya Sorokina produced the exhibitions and artists' residencies that enabled me to make many of these works. Thank you to Elizabeth Maclennan for bringing such panache and intelligence to the voice-over in *Capital*. Thank you to Elena Dobrashkus and Zinovy Zinik for translating *Capital* into Russian so brilliantly, allowing it to be appreciated in Central Asia and Russia. Yuliya Sorokina I have to thank many times over, for her hospitality in Almaty, for introducing me to Kazakhstan and to artists there, for being such a good friend, and for helping me realise each and every project I have filmed in Kazakhstan. I am hugely grateful to the many friends, colleagues and acquaintances who have shared their stories, experiences and expertise with me and have inspired and contributed to the making of the works described in this book.

Lastly, I thank all my family, and Robin especially, for inspiring, supporting and encouraging me in every way.

For my parents,
Helen and Bob Maclennan

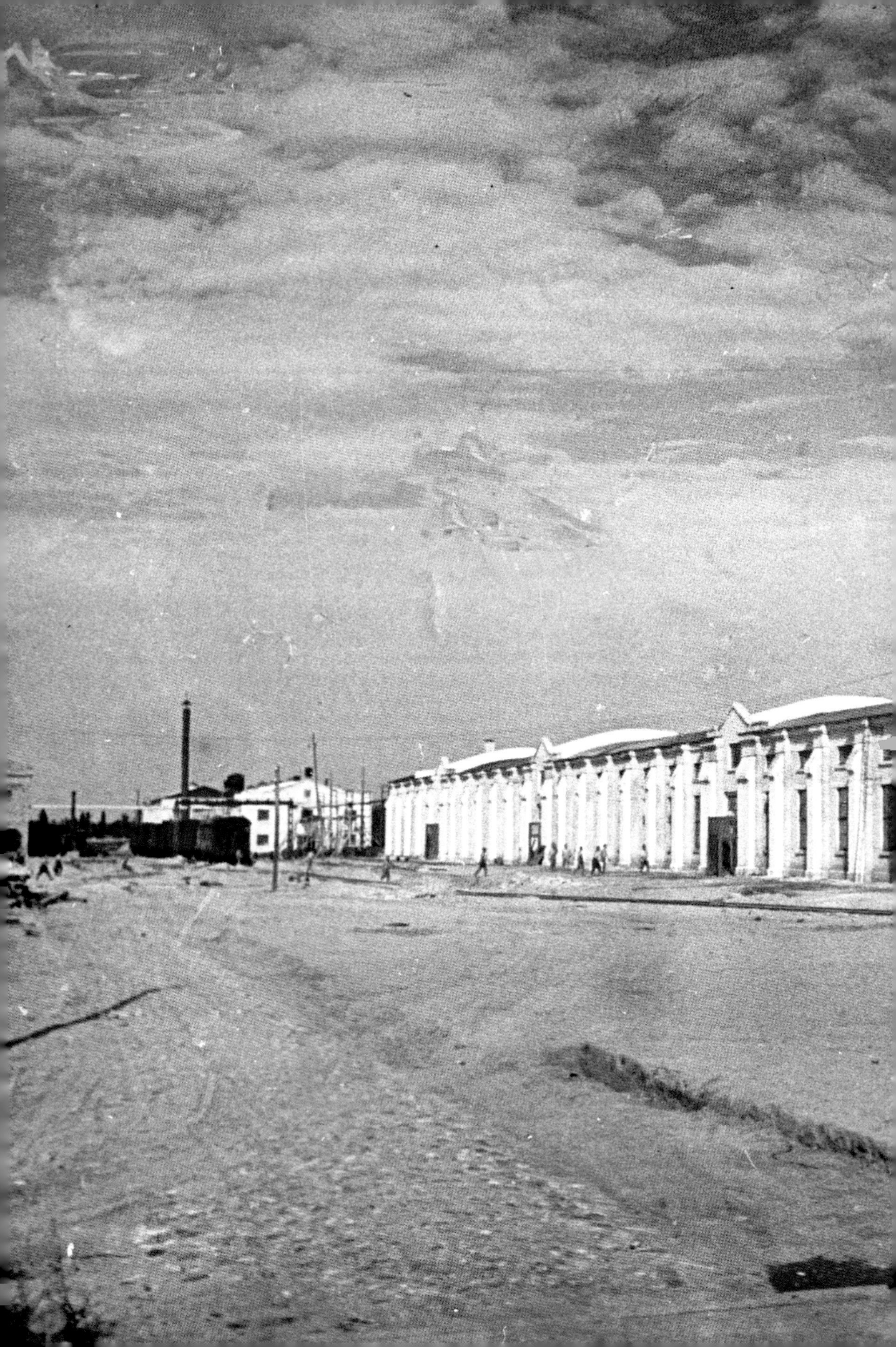

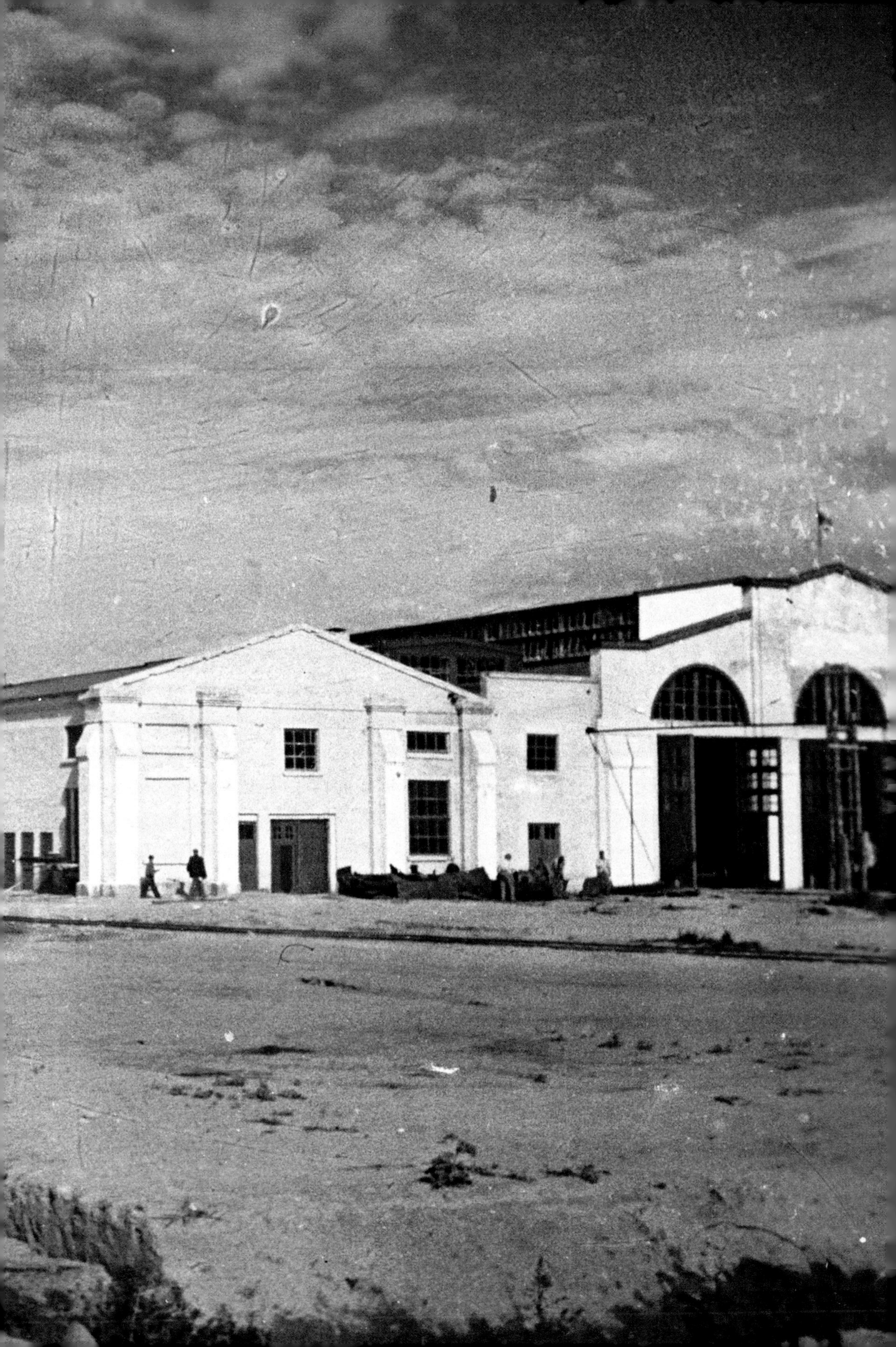

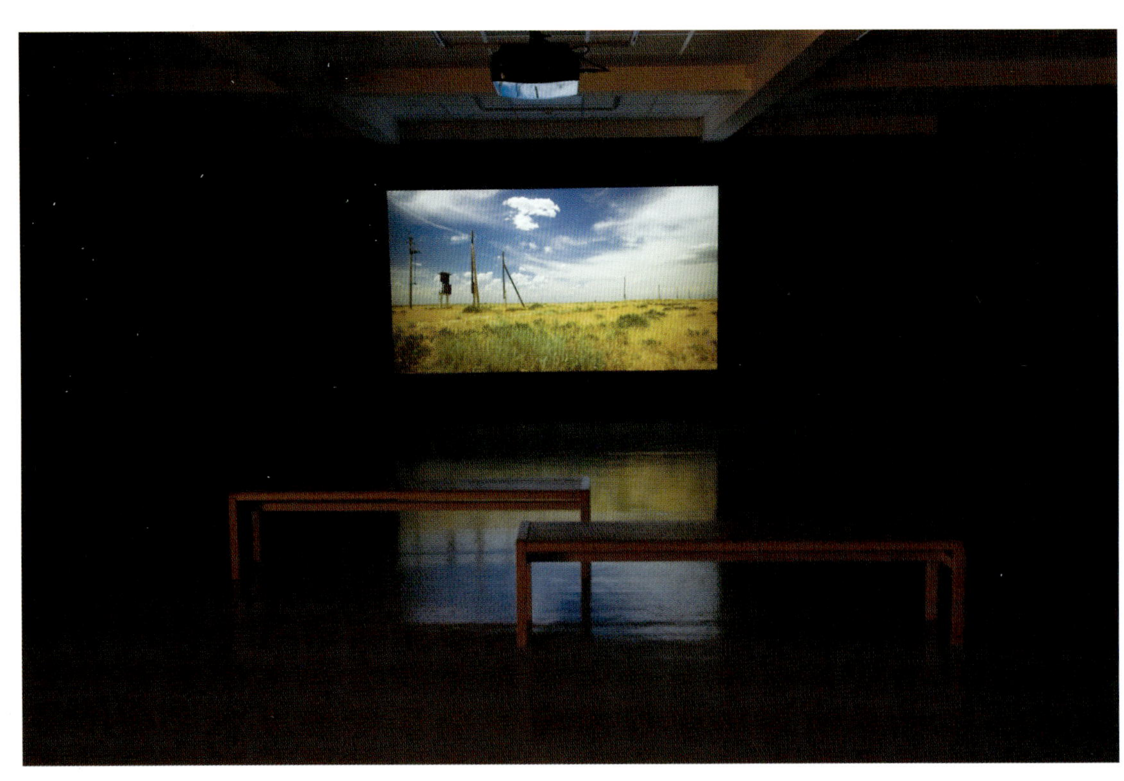

FOREWORD

STEPHEN FOSTER and STEVEN BODE

Ruth Maclennan's *Anarcadia* is the latest in a series of film and video projects that John Hansard Gallery and Film and Video Umbrella have commissioned together in a highly productive collaborative relationship that now stretches back almost two decades. Maclennan's most ambitious and, arguably, her most sophisticated and accomplished work to date, *Anarcadia* is itself the latest in a cluster of film and video pieces that she has shot in the former Soviet Republic of Kazakhstan, charting her encounter with its distinctive landscape and its equally singular history. A haunting meditation on the passing of time and the materialities of place, *Anarcadia* is an impressive achievement that is testimony to Maclennan's feeling for images — and her way with words. Unfolding over a procession of set-piece scenes whose cinematic iconography belies a delicate, poetic intimacy, the video's parallel monologues (voiced by its pair of iconic, almost duelling protagonists) have a subtlety and a fluency that is exceptionally rare in artists' projects.

Ruth's deftness with language and her facility and sensitivity for ideas has made this a particularly stimulating project to work on. Her ambitions for the piece have also necessitated a much wider collaboration, with partners in Kazakhstan, as well as in the UK. In Kazakhstan, the British Council Office in Almaty (particularly Maya Zedelashvili) offered invaluable support for the filming, which also benefitted greatly from the energy and contacts of Yulia Sorokina. We would like to thank our commissioning partners — Ffotogallery, Stills and Castlefield Gallery — for their commitment to *Anarcadia*, and its companion photographic works. Our thanks go also to Arts Council England and the Henry Moore Foundation for their financial support. Working closely with Ruth, the designer Simon Josebury has given shape to a publication whose finesse and attention to detail mirrors and complements its subject. On behalf of our colleagues at Film and Video Umbrella and John Hansard Gallery, we would like to thank everyone involved for making this such an enjoyable experience.

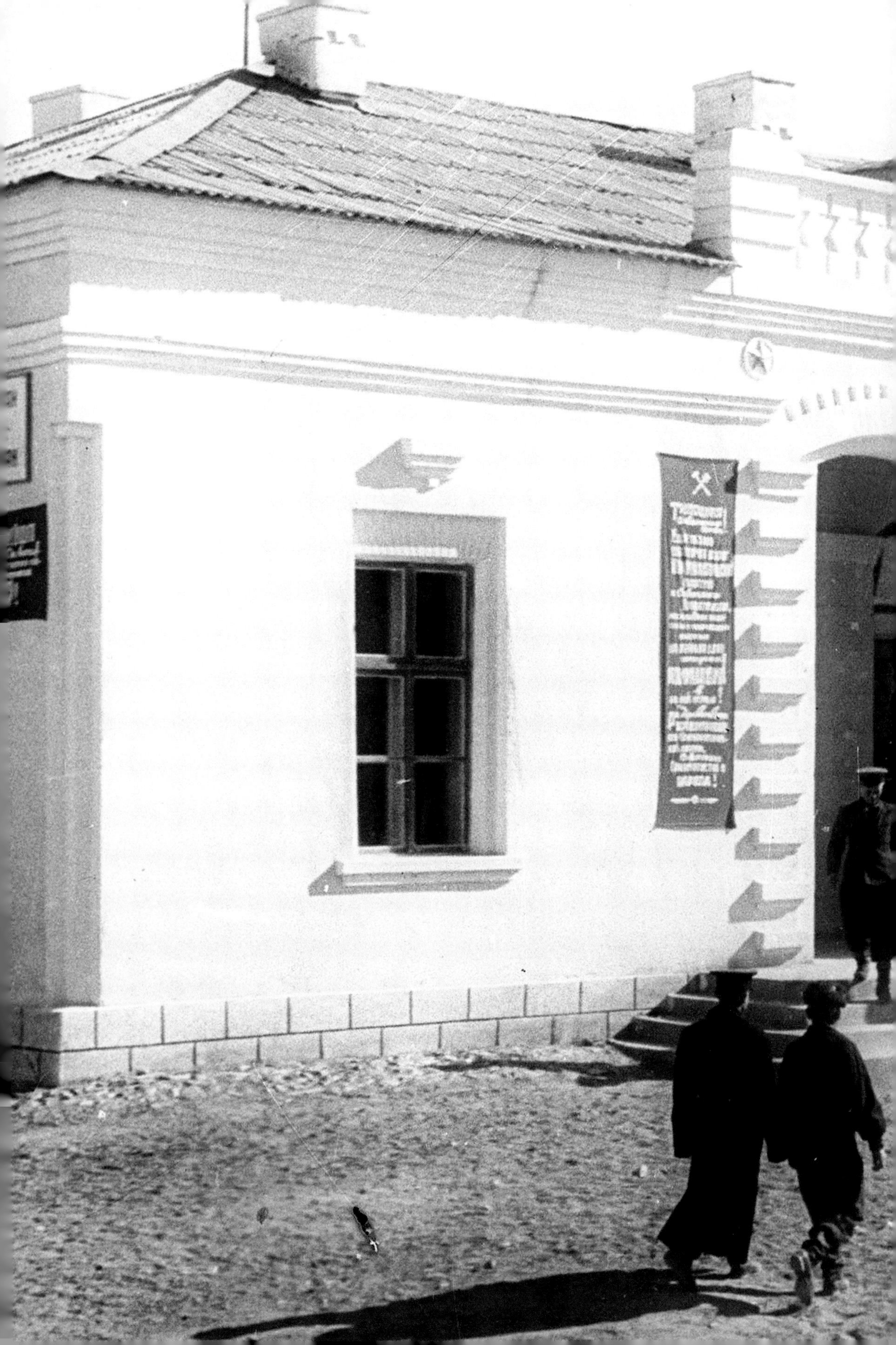

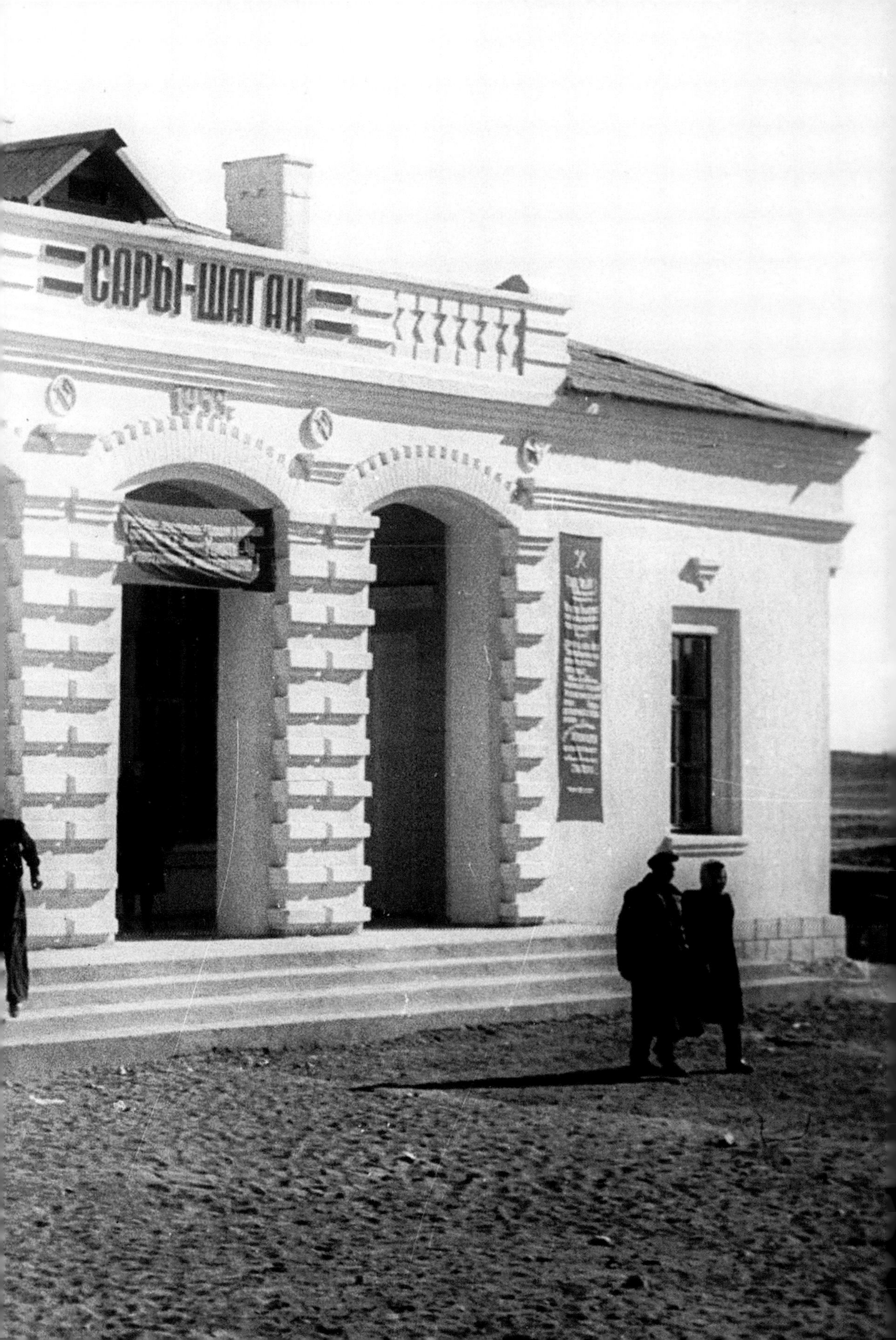
САРЫ-ШАГАН
1953г.

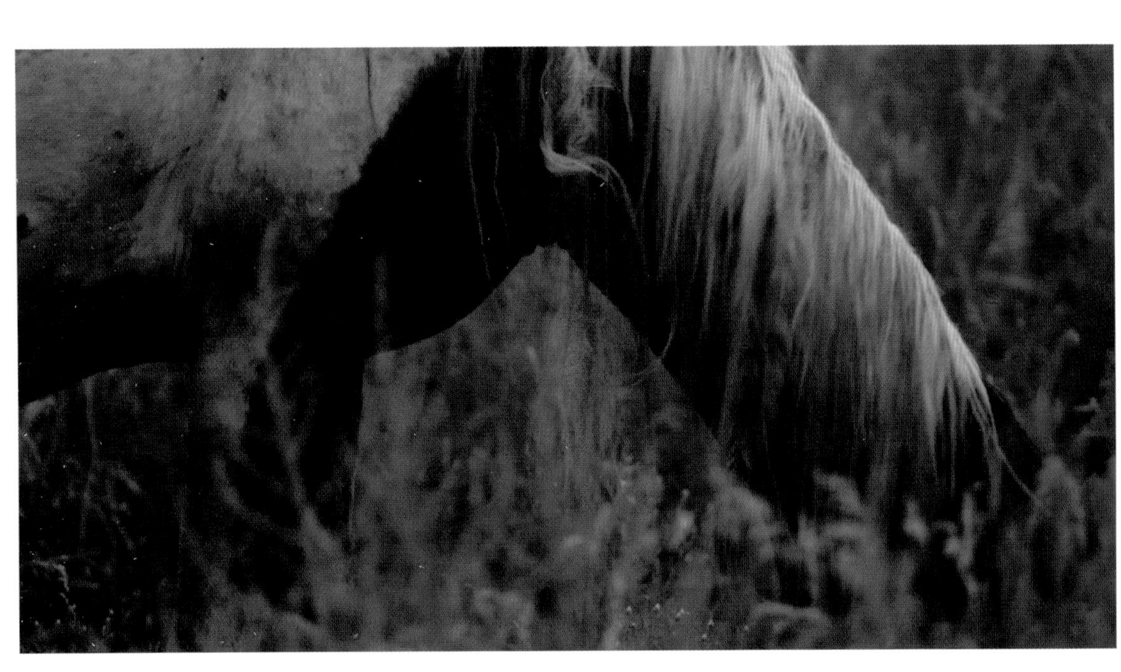

DISPOSABLE CAPITAL

STEVEN BODE

For almost all of their history, the Kazakh people have been nomads, eking out a pastoral existence on the vast expanses of the central Asian steppe. Whether out of a need to stay ahead of the dessicating winds that swiftly turn the prairie to desert, or in the belief that the grass is always greener over the horizon, they have seldom stopped in one spot for long. Where other civilisations founded settlements, raising the glittering cities that became their apotheosis, the Kazakhs had their yurts — rudimentary tents made of felt that they carried with them as they went. Treading lightly upon the earth, so lightly that the grass retained only the most temporary traces of their passing, the rhythms and patterns of these ancestral wanderings are indelibly imprinted on the Kazakh psyche; so deeply engrained as to be part of their collective unconscious. In all this restless motion (following the natural grazing of their livestock, or riding the wild horses of the region to the far-flung frontiers of their world) the steppe has presented an endless, inexhaustible vista. It is the Kazakhs' spiritual heartland; a place of myth and a field of dreams.

The steppe may have sustained this nomadic way of life for untold generations, but it is what lies beneath its surface that has conferred material prosperity. Oil, gas and mineral deposits, in extraordinary abundance, have generated unprecedented wealth; much of it increasingly concentrated in the hands of a new class of oligarchs, with close ties to the government. This embarrassment of riches seems to have encouraged equally exorbitant aspirations for the new independent nation-state of Kazakhstan. Where once a tribal leader would have erected a ceremonial yurt, and gathered his people around him, the country's current ruler, Nursultan Nazarbayev, has elected to pitch a whole new capital in the wide open spaces of the so-called Virgin Lands. (As possible testament to this act of immaculate creation, as if restoring the prelapsarian bond between words and things, the name Astana means, simply, 'capital'). A stately pleasure dome, magicked out of nothing by presidential decree, Astana's fairy-tale aspect is enhanced by its futuristic fantasy architecture. With money no object, and a licence to indulge the imagination, Nazarbayev has gone out of his way to attract the foremost international talent, and has been rewarded with a showpiece metropolis: part architectural playground, part expo for his new-model Kazakhstan.

Ruth Maclennan's video *Capital*, filmed in Astana in 2005, is addressed to a fictional 'prince', whose penchant for trophy buildings and escalating symptoms of folie de grandeur carry echoes of Shelley's Ozymandias. Inspired by her second visit to the country, Maclennan's reflections on transformation and illusion, and the fine line between ambition and hubris, reverberate powerfully against the backdrop of Astana's latterday Xanadu but also apply equally trenchantly to a growing number of asset-rich economies that, in a spiral of one-upmanship, have each conjured spectacular oases from the desert. Like Dubai, or Las Vegas, or mythological Babylon, Astana is a place of conspicuous consumption and ostentatious display — a capital of surplus (and occasional excess) that owes its existence, in almost every aspect, to a corresponding surplus of capital. As with equivalent architectural marvels, the skies above the desert have been brilliantly illuminated, but only by expending its natural resources; so gushingly plentiful that they are almost disposable.

Maclennan's most recent film *Anarcadia* is an obvious companion piece to *Capital*. A cinematic counterpoint to that subtle and discursive video essay, it is set where the Kazakh steppe fringes onto the desert, and follows two emblematic characters: an archaeologist and a prospector. Looking beyond the lie of the land for what is hidden underneath, the duo's paths converge in a dilapidated way-station of a former colonial railway; now abandoned, and leading nowhere. In this desolate outpost of the old Soviet empire, the ghosts of barely-remembered ancient societies are invoked; each, in turn, made to seem all the more fleeting by the presence of the adamantine rocks that have shaped this stark and elemental landscape. Beguiled by its Utopian spirit of place, while also alluding to the free-market goldrush frenzy of the post-Soviet era (neatly encapsulated in the wordplay of the title), *Anarcadia* uncovers some of the historical, cultural and psychological impulses at play in contemporary Kazakhstan. It also offers a reminder how, for all the wealth some people may have at their disposal in the pursuit of a lasting legacy, when compared to the passage of history and the span of geological time, the marks we leave on the world around us are little more than transitory.

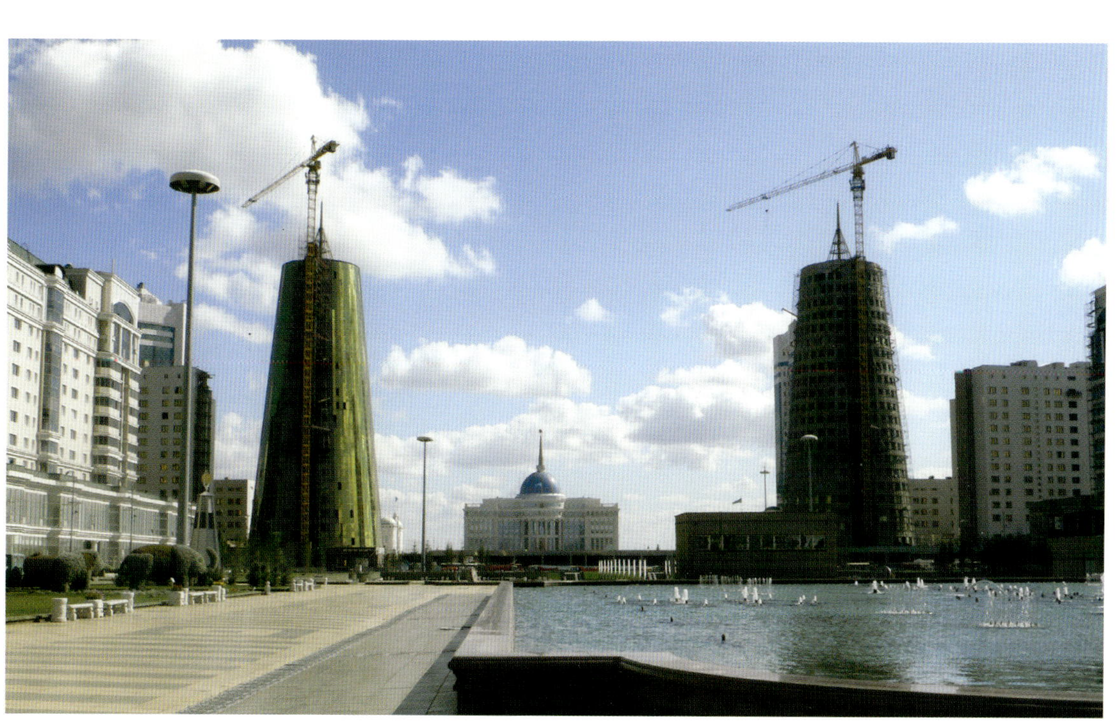

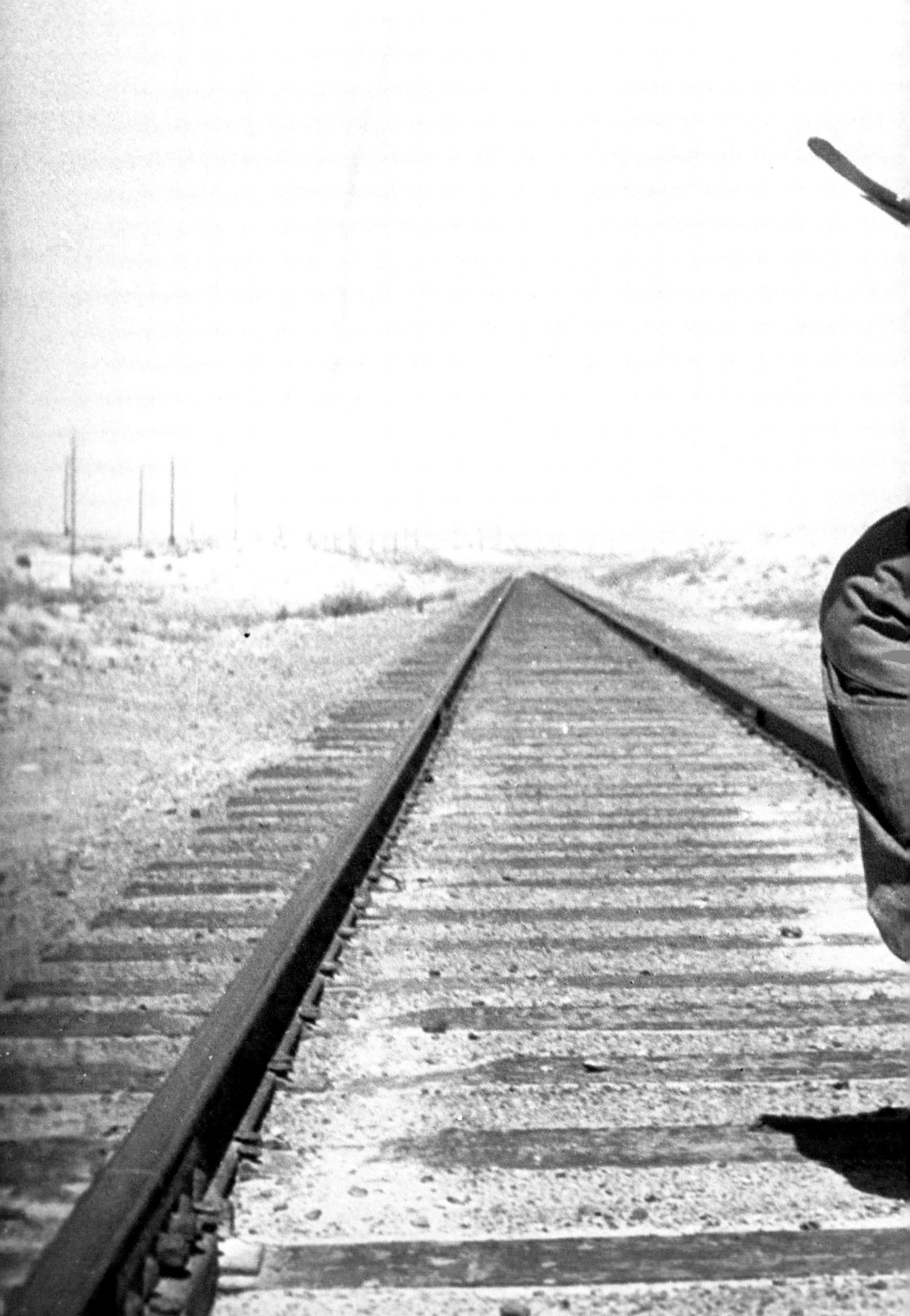

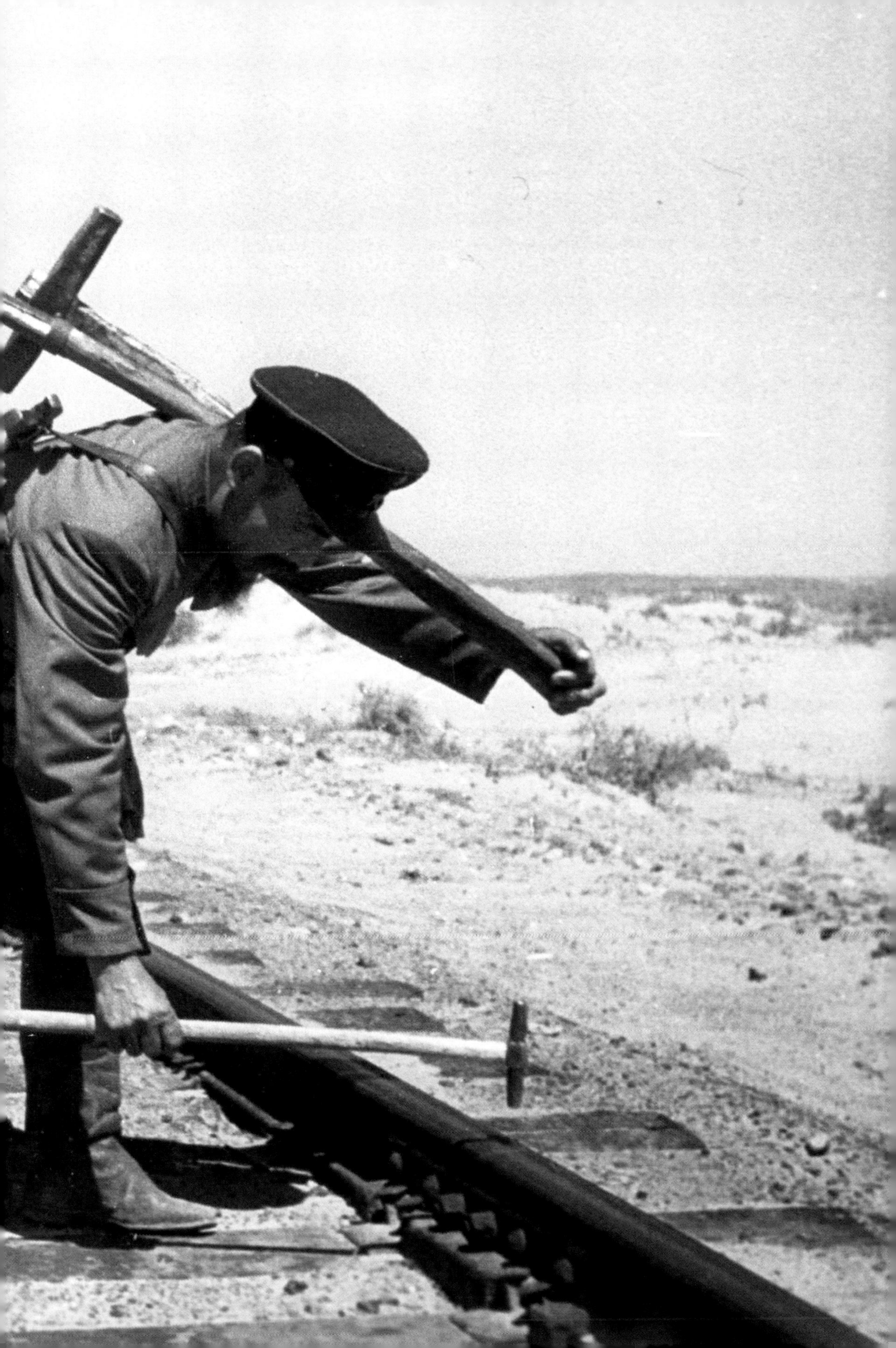

During the first three days' march, the impressive, endless silence of the desert — a silence as of the grave — cast a most powerful spell over my soul. Often did I stare vacantly for hours, my eyes fixed on the distance before me, and as my companions believed me to be sunk in religious meditations, I was very seldom disturbed.

…Taken as the whole, these Asiatic steppes were always, as far back as the memory of man goes, howling wildernesses. The vast tracts which stretch for many days' journey without one drop of drinkable water, the expanses many hundred miles in extent of deep loose sand, the extreme violence of the climate, and such like obstacles, defy even modern art and science to cope with them.

Sketches of Central Asia, Arminius Vambery, 1868

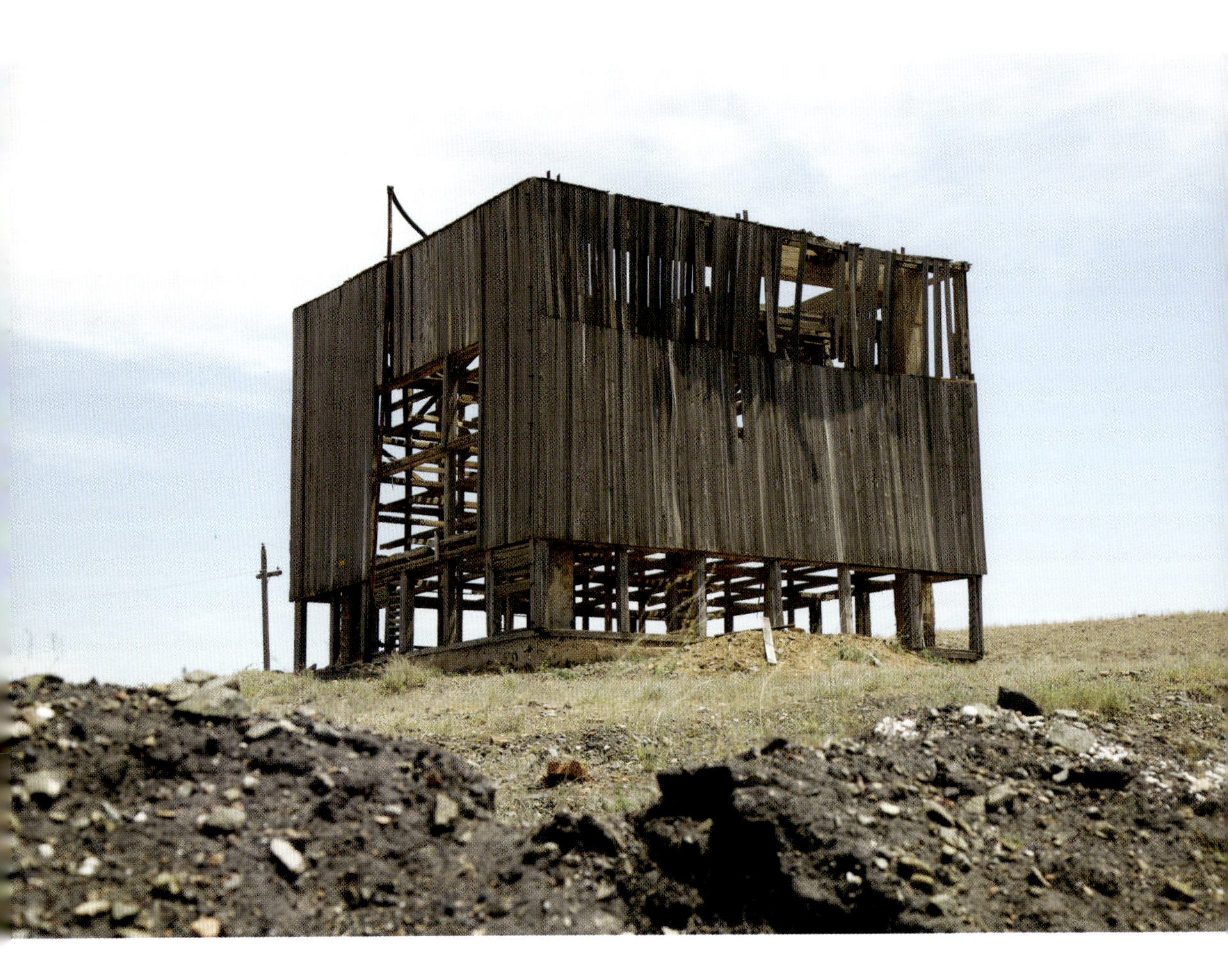

ANARCADIA

SCREENPLAY

PROSPECTOR: Forward... Back. Stop. Begin again.
I'll stay a while. Something may turn up. One day.
One day. One night... Two days. Three weeks. Four years. Five decades.
Six hundred years. Seven thousand years. Eight million years. Nine billion
years. Ten light years. From now... Back a bit. Back a bit. Back a bit. From
here. Here. From here.
I like to count my steps. To know where I'm going, how far I've been.
Forward... Back. Stop. Begin again.
I'll stay a while. Something may turn up. one day.
One day. One night... two days. Three weeks. Four years. Five decades.
Six hundred years. Seven thousand years. Eight million years. Nine billion
years. Ten light years. From now... Back a bit. Back a bit. Back a bit. From
here. Here. From here. I like to count my steps. To know where I'm going,
how far I've been.

[sound carried away on the wind]
Sand is good. It softens your landing when you fall. And no one ever needs
to know you did.

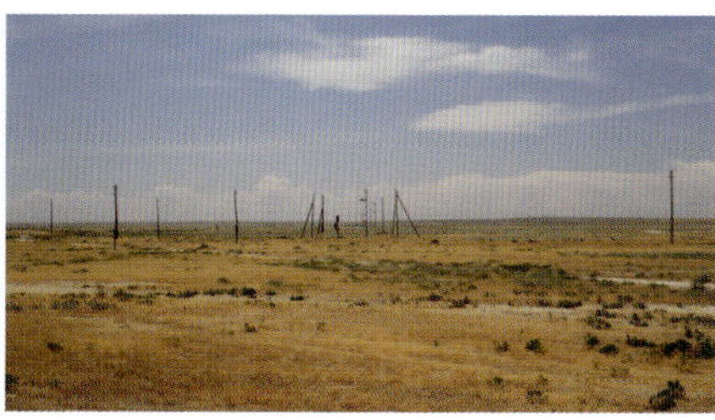
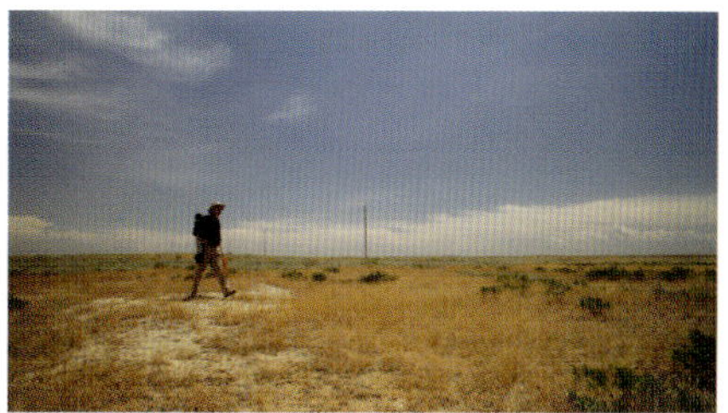

ARCHAEOLOGIST: I have heard that this was going to be the capital of the country, and that a railway station was built, though no tracks were ever laid. Who can tell me what happened? The land itself doesn't speak.
There is nothing to stop you from walking. Nothing to interrupt your view back, back, back, in time. There is no back or forward. Only up... and down... What time are we talking about anyway? The time when it mattered is over now. This place was finished long before the station, before the people who took it apart, last week, or last year.
Horses brought people here, ten thousand years ago.
Whose story was it? It was stolen and no one wrote down where it was put. Here lived an exiled people, close to the ground.

[voice-over]
They dragged themselves across the surface of the earth. Their breath gathered dust. Their words hung there, waiting to be picked up again, or to sink into the ground out of sight.

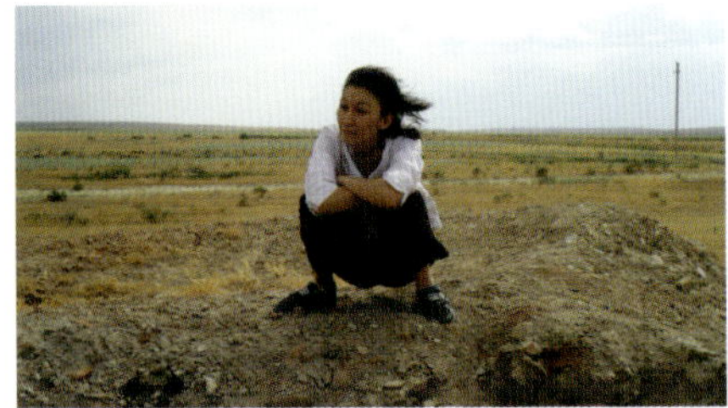

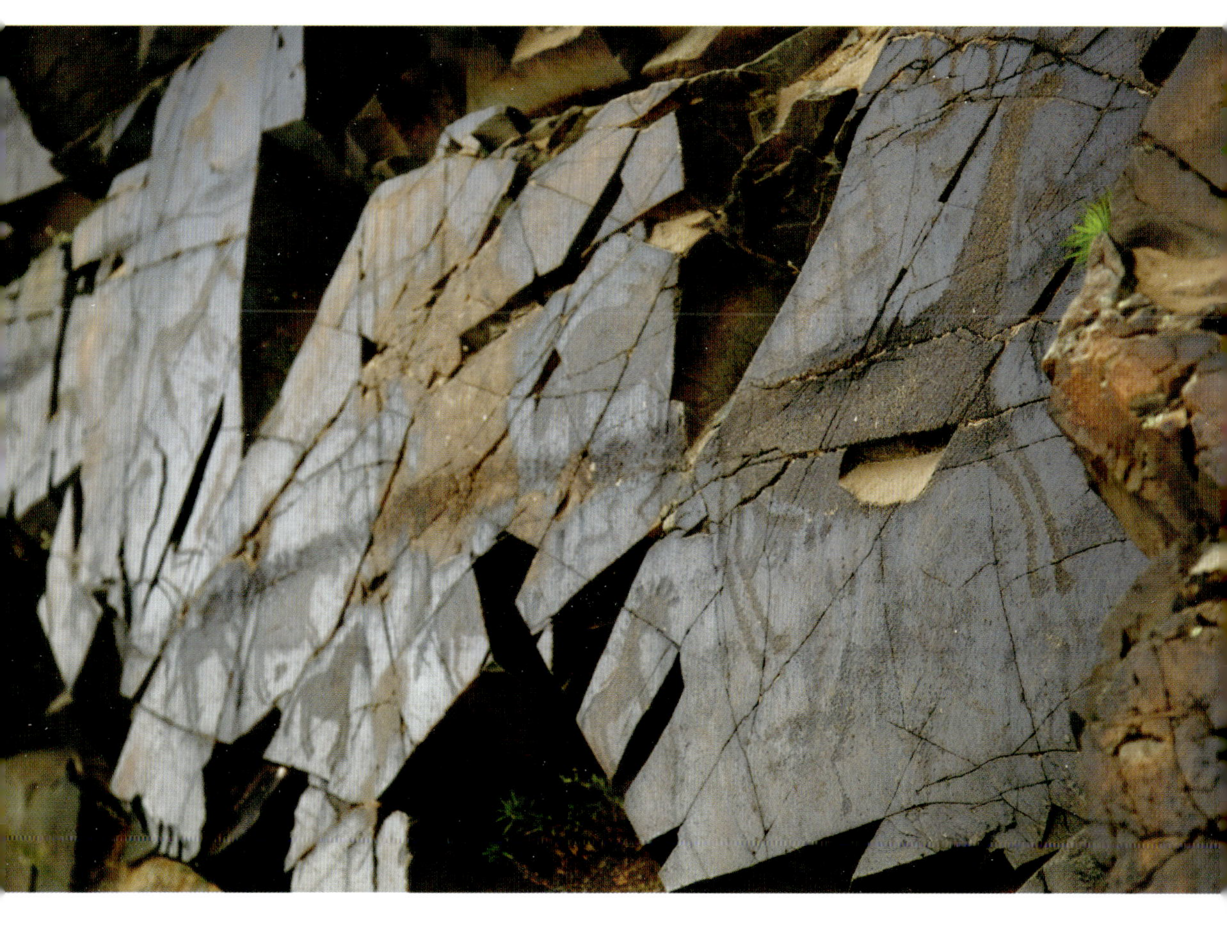

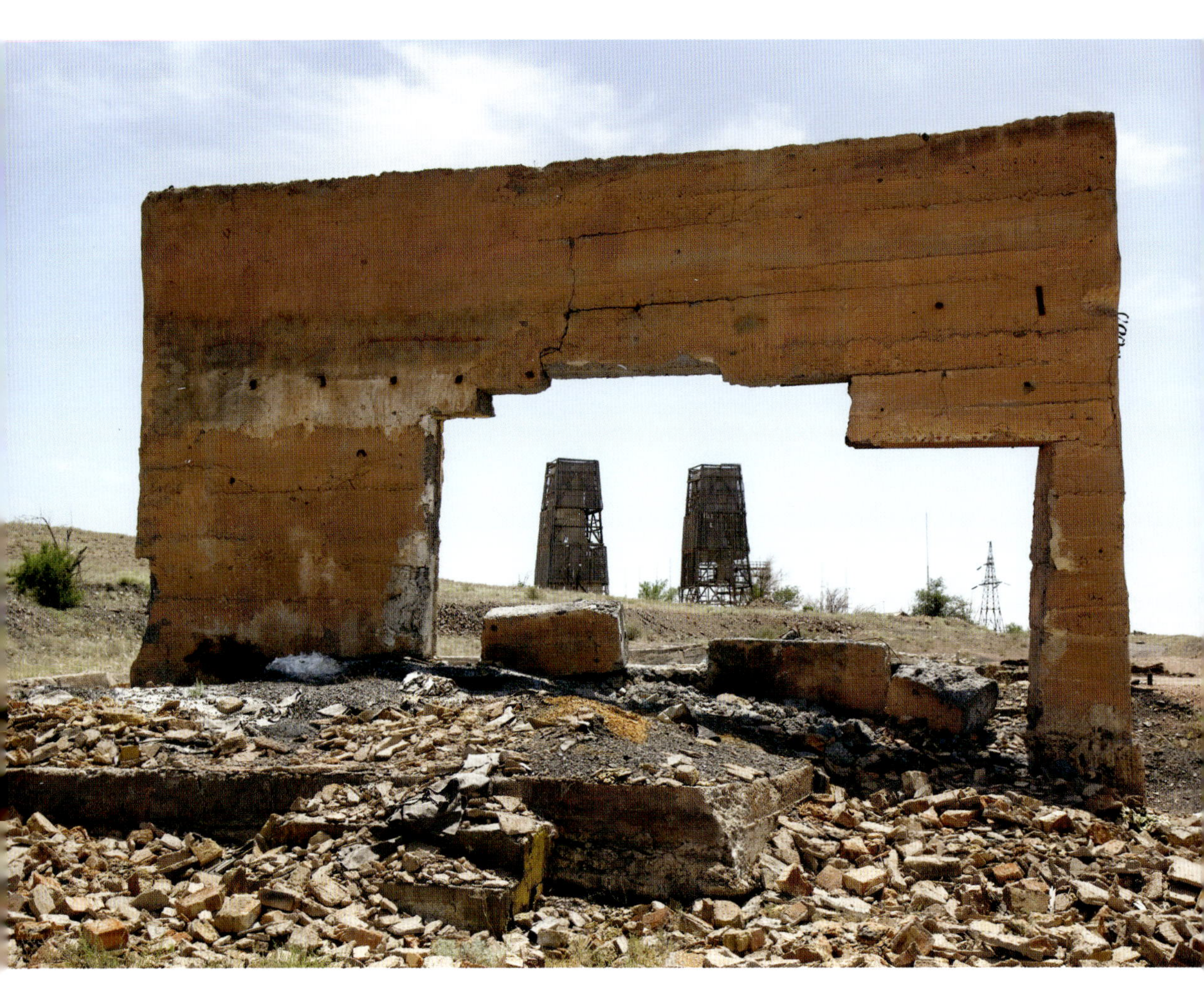

PROSPECTOR: The simplest would be methane: one atom of carbon, four of hydrogen. Round and round you go, covering every inch, pounding the ground, sending signals into the earth. Nothing to interrupt you. You've got to keep going. It'll all be worth it eventually, or over soon.

I have been here a year now. I've eaten nothing but air and sand.
I met a man who kept a stone in his mouth for three years, just to teach himself to keep shtum.
A goat. A camel.
A hammer. The birds. The birds. A horse. Ten horses. A warm cloth.
A snake. Three white horses. One black horse. A kite.
One step. Two steps. Three steps. Four.

I am a prospector. I deal in prospects, views, expectations, and directions. Unproven, but against what?
A prospect can succeed or fail. One prospect, two prospects, a thread of them, beads on a string of hopes and plans. Now, to build a business case for drilling: you need a portfolio of choices.
I've forgotten why I am here.

[voice-over]
I am the first person to see this buried cube of world.

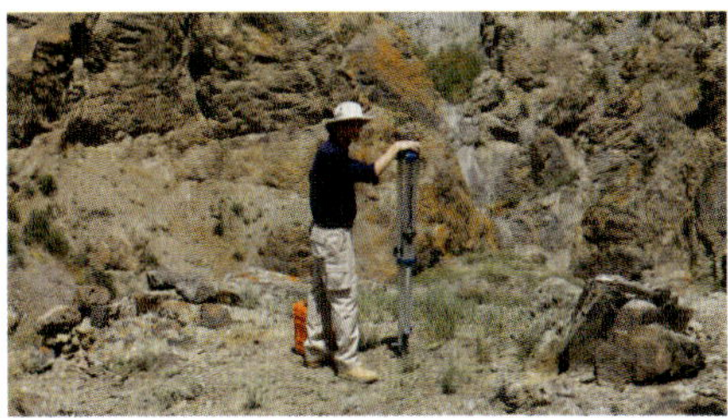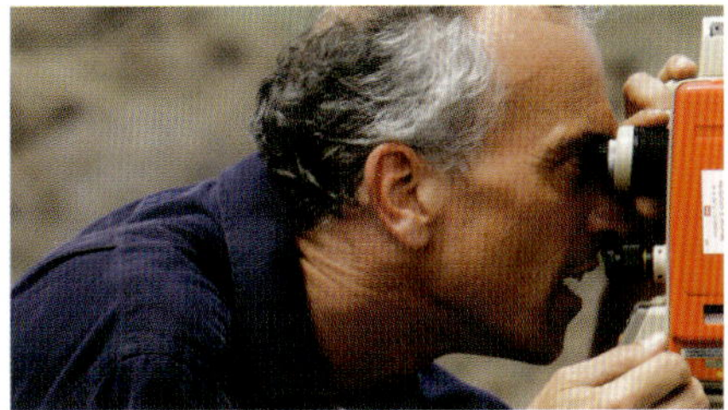

ARCHAEOLOGIST: What happened to the capital? The capital that wasn't, that won't be, that will be again, and then will disappear again. I want to touch the capital, the flickering moment when the focus was on this spot, when the flame scorched this earth. Ten thousand years ago. Or fifty or ninety.

[voice-over]
Time of birth, more births, more and more, and deaths and births again and again and again, until the deaths outdo the births and then there is no more of it. That's the end of that time.

But maybe something remained, perhaps someone, somewhere, or something, very small, easily hidden, living on air, living on grass, carrying the story, carried on somehow, and told the story to someone, or carved it into camel skin, or horse bone, or rock even, or maybe just wrote it in the sand.

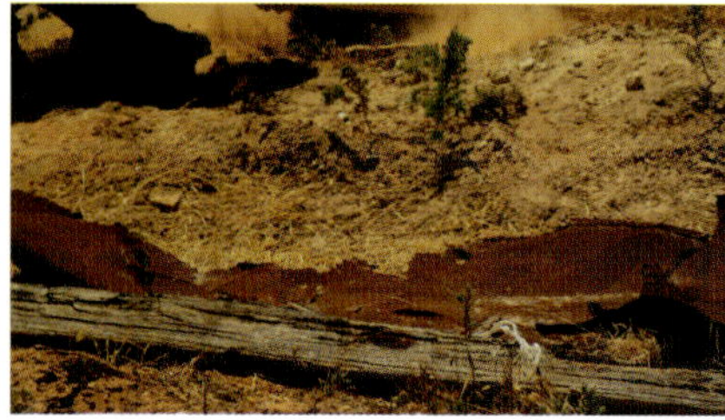
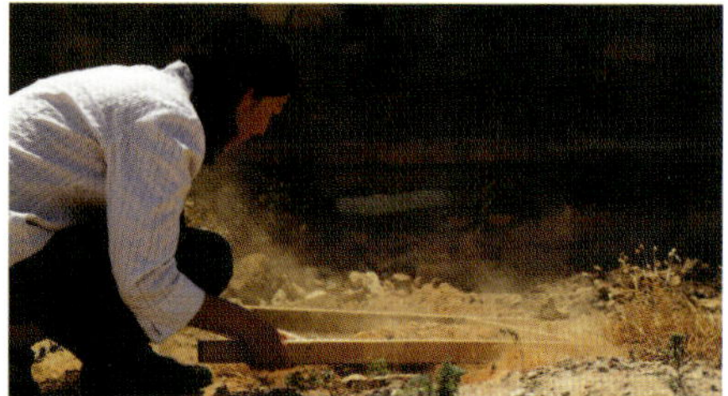

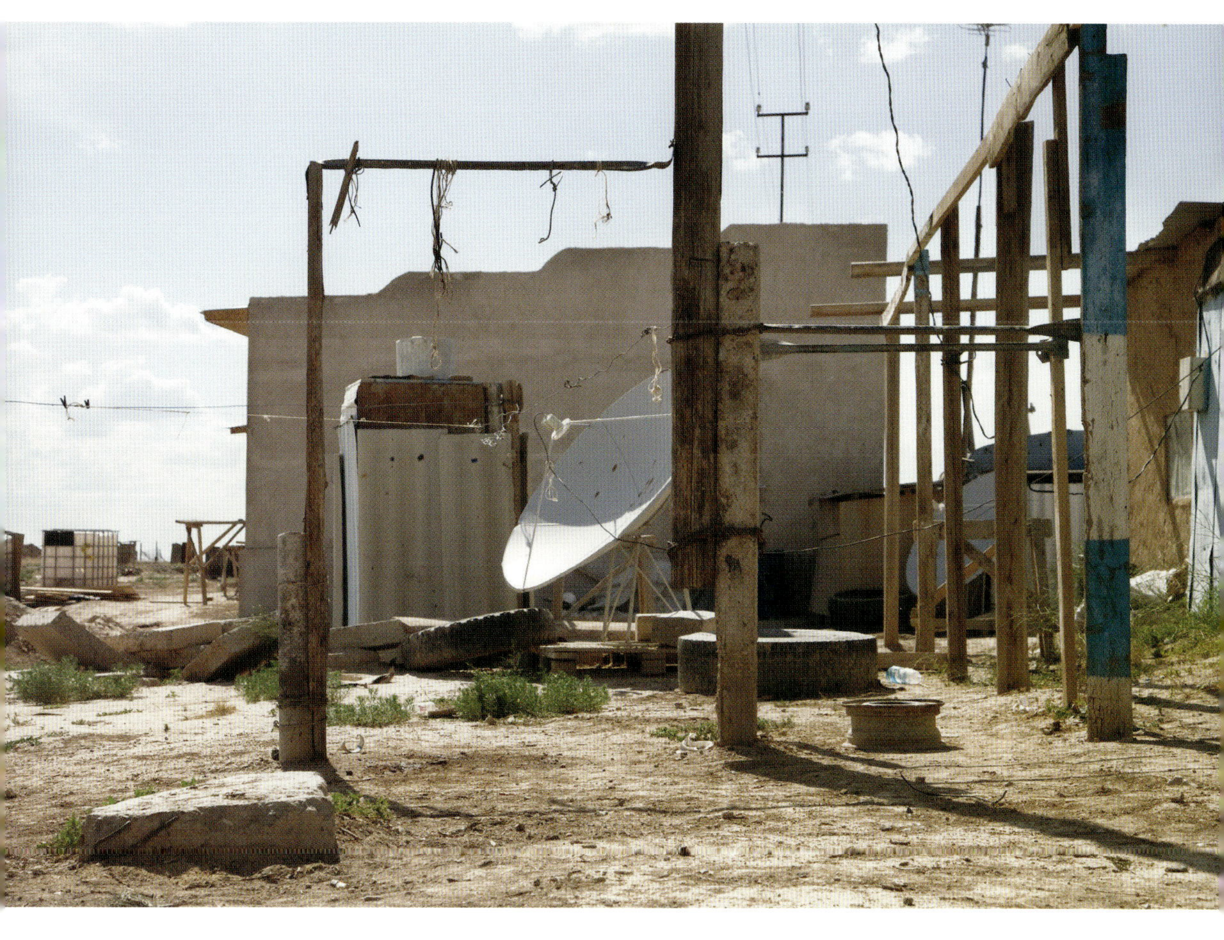

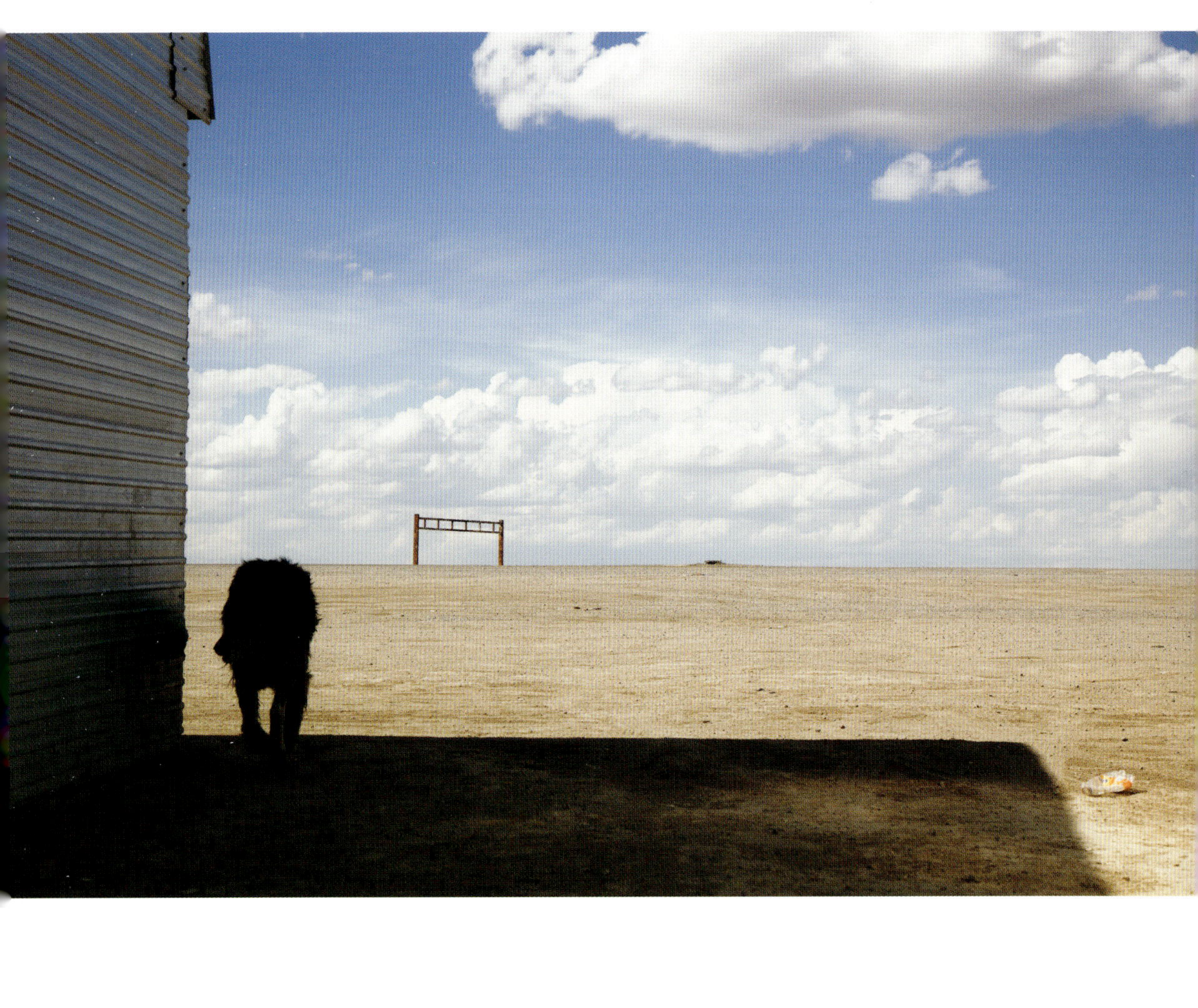

PROSPECTOR: *[voice-over]*

I came here years ago when it was empty. I made a fortune, but now it's used up. I was someone else. I left him behind. He's buried somewhere.

[voice-over]

If you wait long enough all life is transformed into rock. And we make that rock live again: cyclocarbons, mono-olefins, and alkenes.

[voice-over]

Diolefins and acetelenes. Naphthalene. Pentanes, isopentanes, cyclohexanes, and aromatics. Stacked, branched, chained, and bonded compounds, sticky, bituminous, waxy. Carbon, hydrogen, oxygen, nitrogen and sulphur

[in picture]

all make life out of rock. Burn into life...and then out again, for good.

[voice-over]

I left then for one reason. I came back for another.
I wanted it all like everyone else, but I didn't want to work for it. Work is for beasts. Work doesn't pay. Waiting pays. Waiting for the right moment, the right promise, the right place. Always on the move, always in the right place, at the right time, with the right people. That takes skill and precision...

I had to leave, to allow the dust to settle. I take the blame, though it wasn't mine to take. I also take the losses.

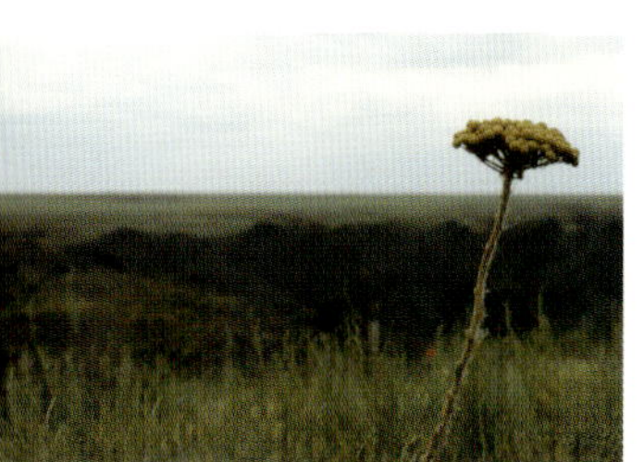
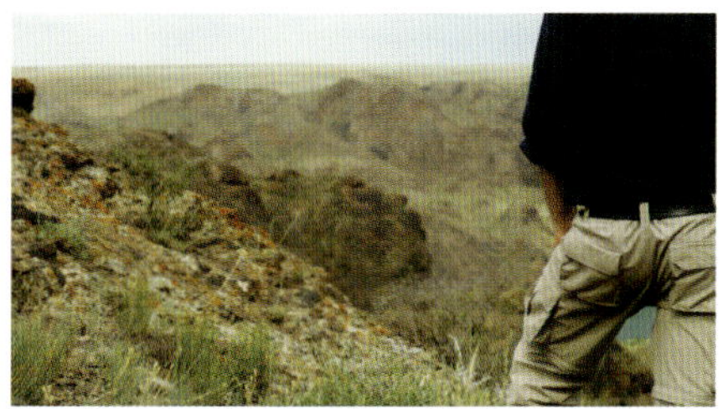
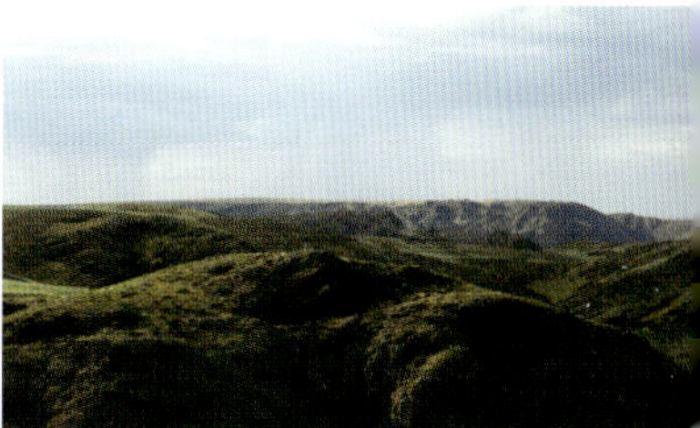

A: Someone told something to someone else...

P: There is one law for the fortunate and another for the unfortunate.

A: and the other took something away,

P: The law for the fortunate is written in sand,

A: and burned a hole and moved on.

P: The law for the unfortunate is written in clay and baked hard. It breaks easily. 'Behind every great fortune lies a great crime.' But the great crime is soon forgotten. People move on. Everyone has to move on, to live with what is. Behind every great fortune lie lots of little fortunes hanging on, waiting for the trickle down, waiting to catch every drip with their mouths wide open. The fountain dries up so best drink from it while you can. The fountain sparkles like a mirror, shows you want to see. Everyone looks into it. If you can't or won't, life is dark.

A: How many vertical lines does it take to make a city? How many horizontal? Are these three houses enough?

They kept speaking of prehistory — wordless time, timeless time. Time began and then what happened? Did people start by writing stories or riding horses? That time didn't disappear, it continued to exist, people moving slowly, and then faster, across the surface of the earth. We've broken off pre-history. We've forgotten how to fashion and grasp a stone tool, how to feel our way across the desert floor, in homes of skin and fat. But what comes next, after prehistory, is also lost: the feel of it, the way of it, the sound of it. Prehistory is just history that hasn't been touched yet — future possibility for the past.

Prehistory will have its time again. It will be post-history.

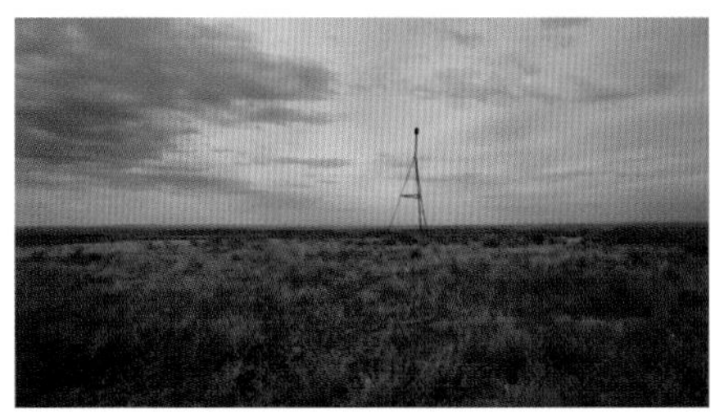

P: Wait and look around. Don't hurry. Keep your eyes open. He's new in town, but he's been here before. He stands still, looking from side to side, hands at the ready. Ready for what? Well, for whatever comes at him. He doesn't know, but doesn't give anything away. That's his business. His reputation precedes him. Wild… horses and tumbleweed, rabbits and sandstone. You name it. Up and over, and off he goes.
His wild may not be your wild.
He's come here for the same reasons as everyone else. Always looks brooding, preoccupied, looking for something more important than what's happening around him right now.
He is looking for something, but not what you think.

[in picture]
I've travelled a hundred thousand miles, and years, from here to Tombstone and back again. From forest and meadow to sand and tumbleweed. A hundred million years, and still nothing may happen.

[voice-over]
The desert has no past, no future, it is all present opportunity.
Back to the beginning, back to the first depositions.

[in picture]
I make maps in time and space, underground; I dismantle the architecture; peel back the layers laid down by rivers; *[voice-over]* push through mountains of sediment dumped at the bottom of canyons. Leaves, fish, trees, mulched and dissolved into organic matter.
Each creature chases pleasure before the order for annihilation is carried out, or postponed once again. But eventually it all becomes rock.

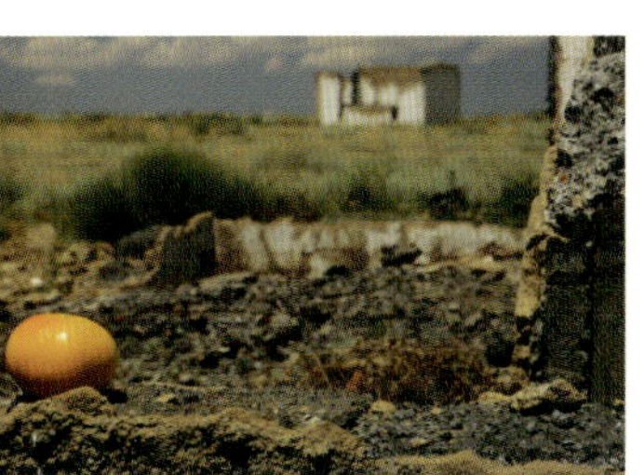
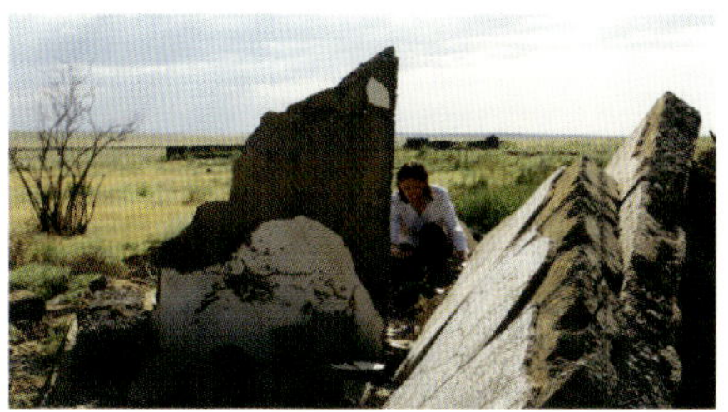
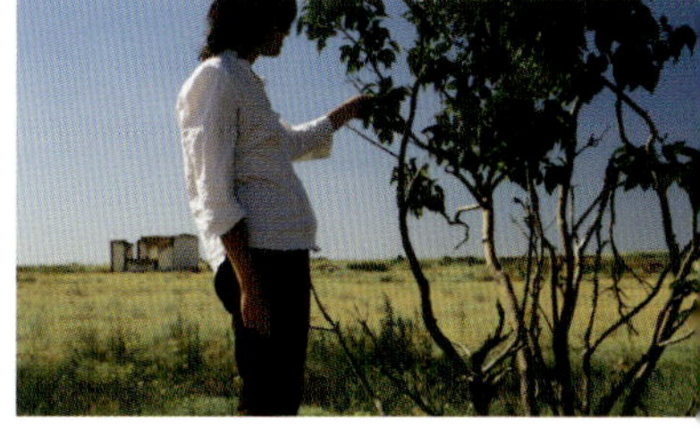

A: I have nothing left to go on. It has all been snatched away from me. But I know how to tell a story.

What are we building here? Once I lived in the future, and now I live in the future of that future. I've chipped away at the rock to find the past, but it isn't there. The past was real, more real than light and dirt, and its absence is real.

We built a dream city here: a dream of kitchen gardens and washing machines, of tomatoes, strawberries and pickles; of fences, porches and children digging holes to bury secrets. Ten and a half square metres of freedom.

You can hear the people leaving. History speeded up, faster than a life-span, to give us back the desert. The water was stolen, siphoned off to sprinkle the dusty Zen gardens of millionaires. Or allowed to drain into the dust while people waited for it to be turned off. A dream of digging plots, resting in the shade. A mirage of nightingales and roses. This is no place for gardens or resting.

P: *[voice-over]*
A band of advisors, speculators, multinationals, oil barons, sex tourists, hikers, bankers, money launderers, Mafiosi, missionaries, spies, financiers and travelling adolescents are the messengers of the future. They'll all end up here.

A: *[in picture — overlapping with the prospector's voice-over]*
The station has gone. The bricks were carried off to build a house or stable. There is still something in the air, I think. In the grass, in the dust and sand

P: You don't look at the desert, it looks at you.

A: … and shadows.

P: You can't sit down in the desert you've got to keep on going.

A: The past is stone and mortar.

P: A man rides into the desert. The desert comes up to him and… bites him in the arse…

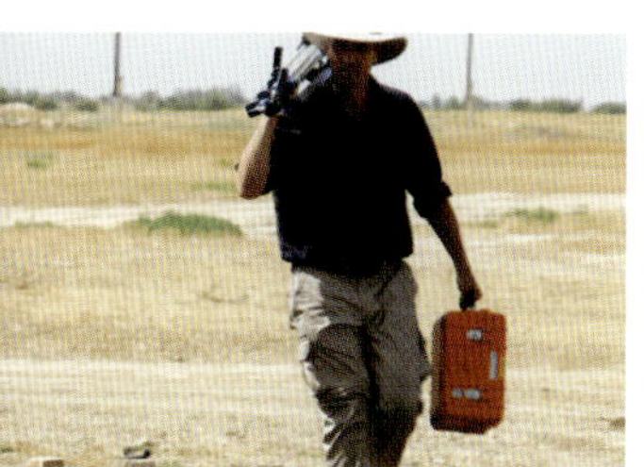
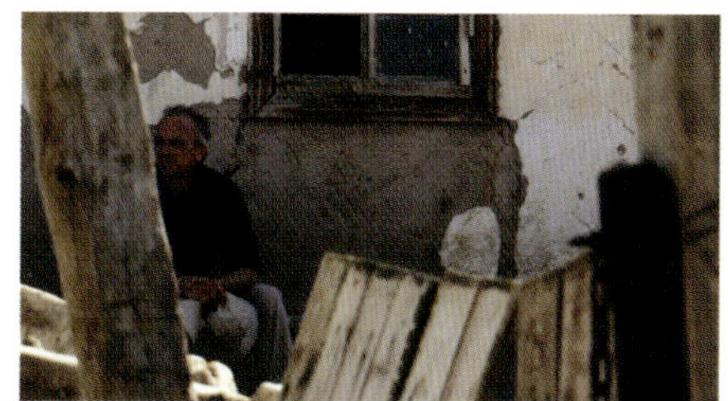
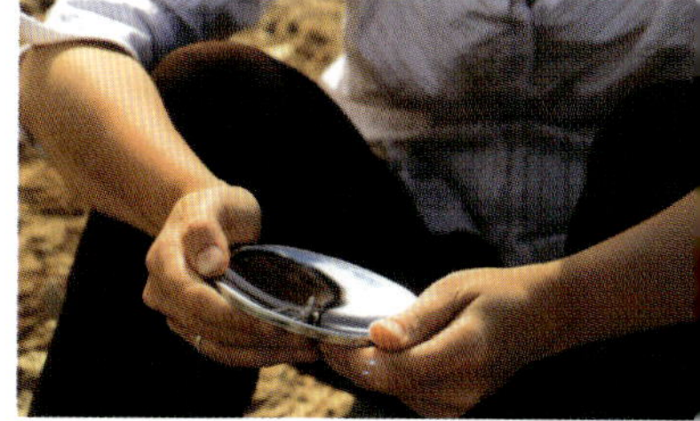

A: It is taken apart and used again, and used again. Dug up, used again, and used, and moved again and again and again. Time to let it lie.

P: ...Or an eagle. Rising on hot air, then wings split the air, the body plummets, beak into neck, and wings cover the prey.

A: I'll find the pieces of the past.

P: A moment to glance about for witnesses, and the head leans over the captive.

A: I'll reassemble them to build a station... With a ticket office, a waiting room, a cafeteria serving strong black tea, and small dry sugary cakes, and greasy soup, a kiosk for cigarettes and sweets, a stationmaster's office, with snapshots of his family, a framed photograph of the smiling leader, posters of green, mountain landscapes and smiling children on holiday. And timetables. I can find the timetables.

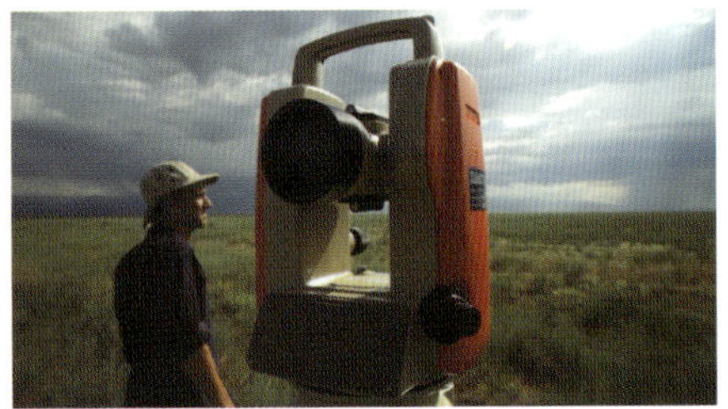

P: Scorpions and spiders live in the desert, but they're gentle when left alone. Their hard shells keep the sand out. Some people can do that too, they survive better in the desert, just like scorpions and spiders. Flesh is so soft and the sand so hard. It drifts. It comes last and smoothes over the destruction.

We are alone at last. Each of us, alone.

If you wait for the East wind and let it blow for a day I will be touching you. This time I am the prospect.

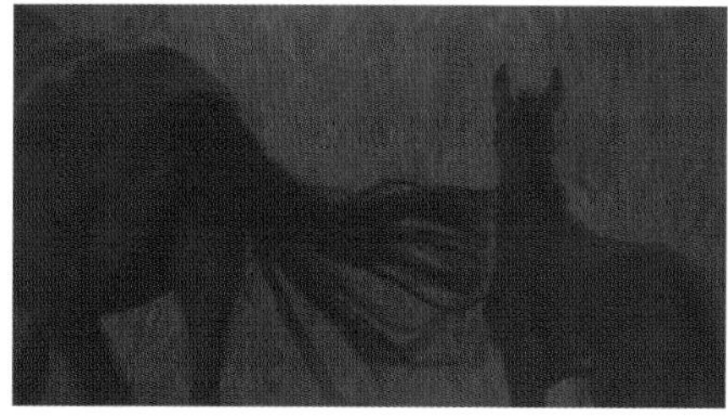 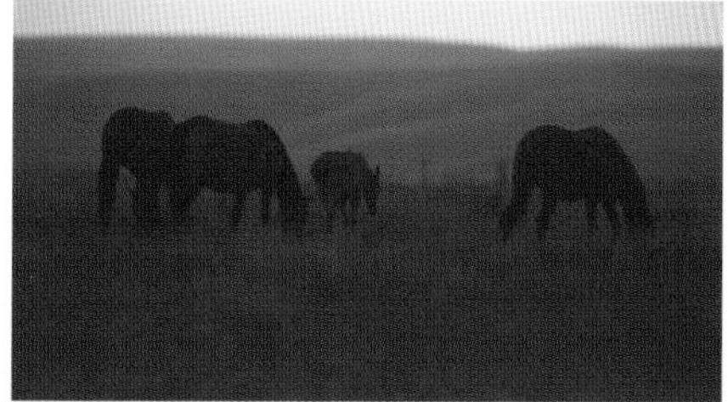

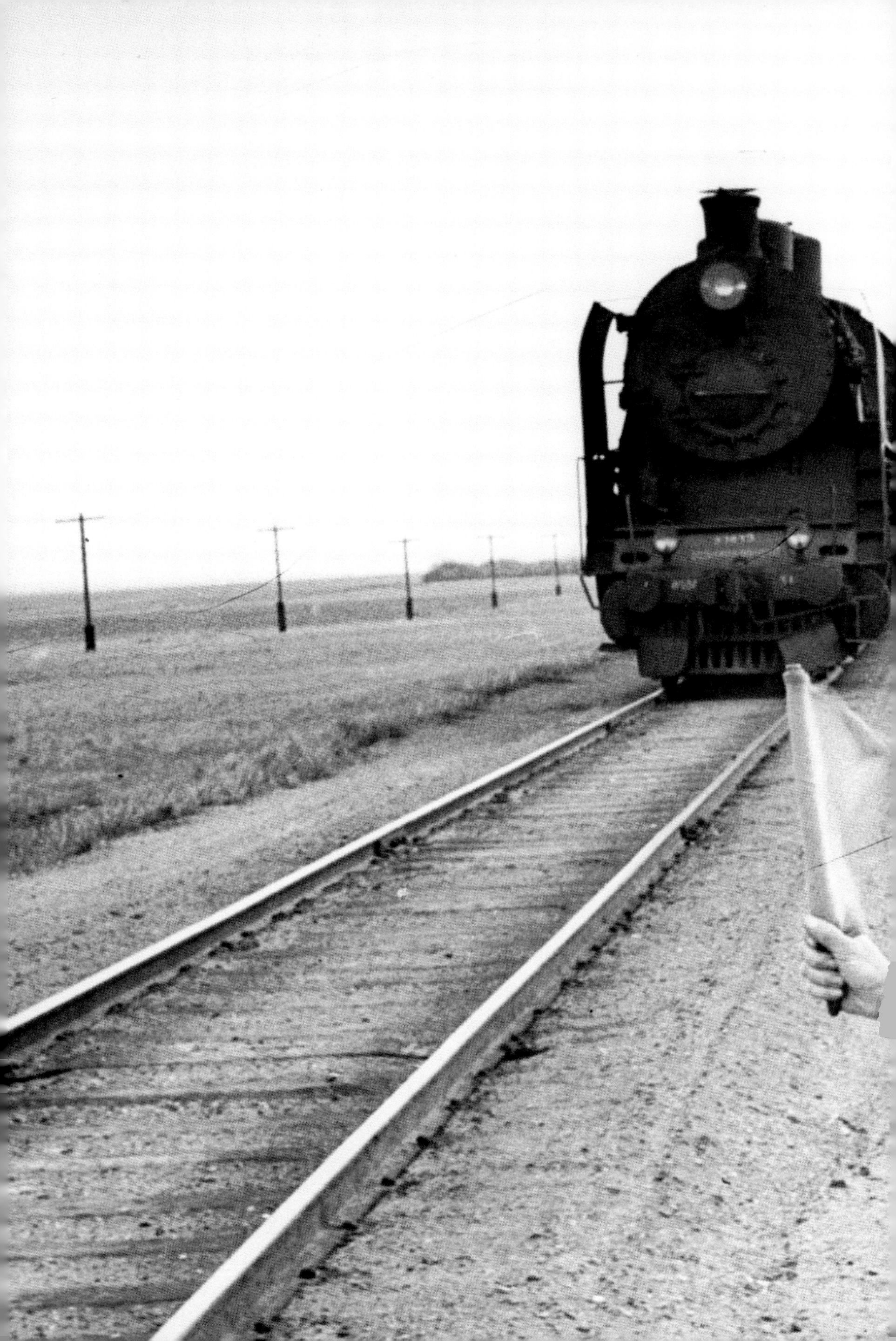

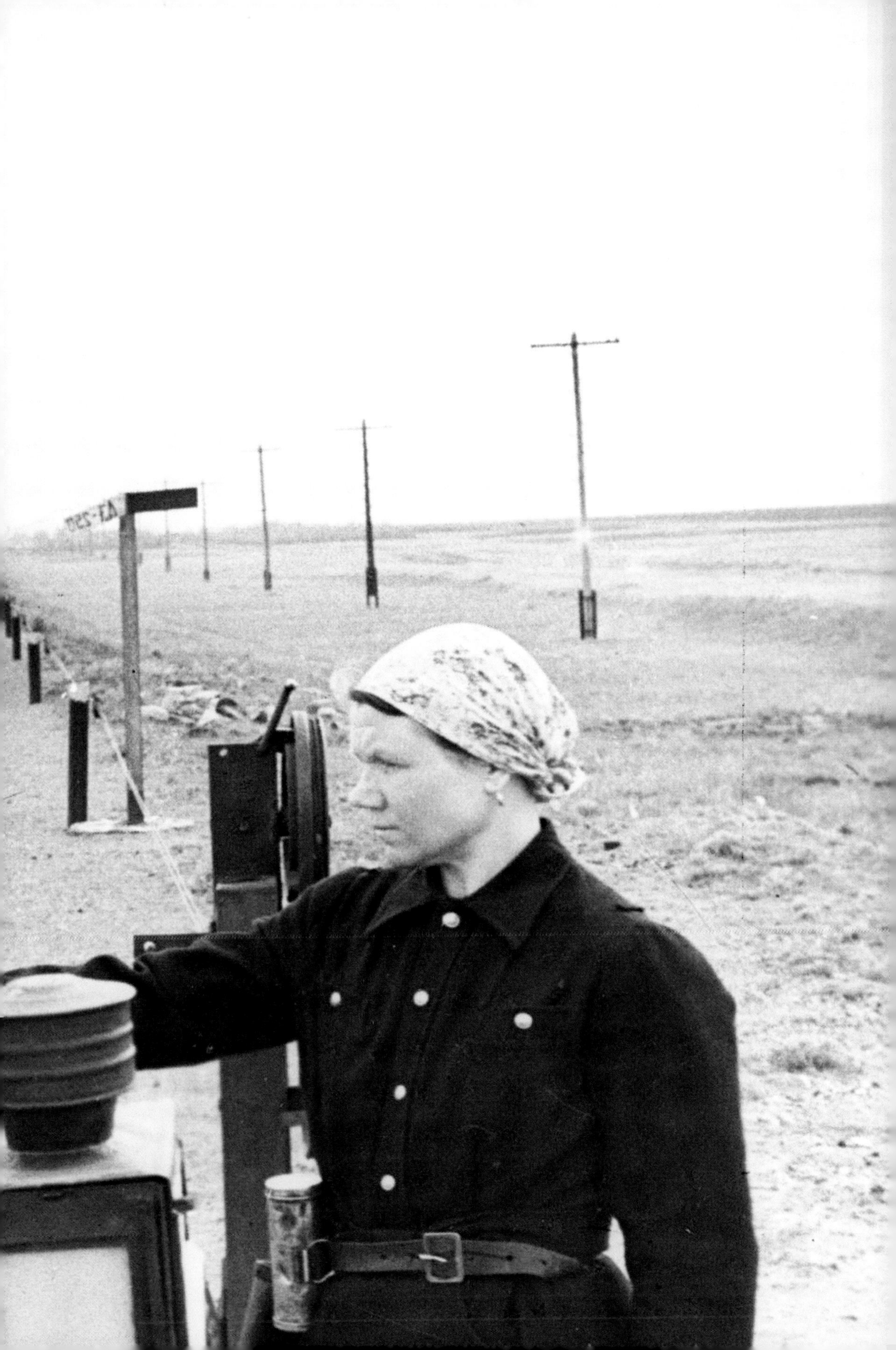

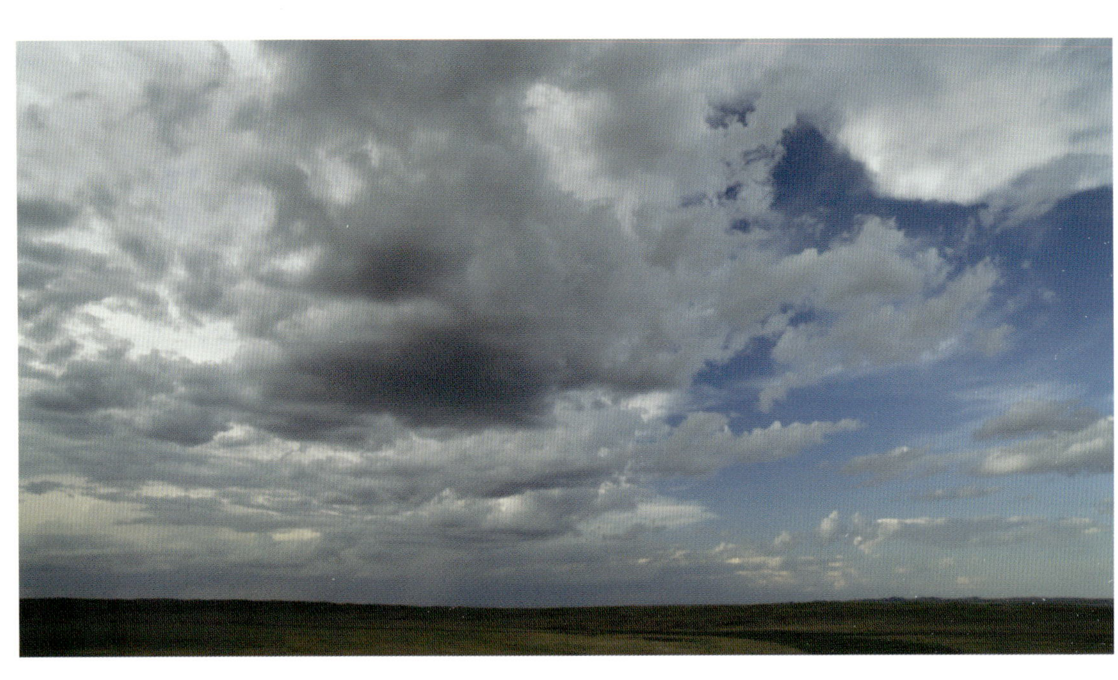

NO PLACE FOR GARDENS OR RESTING

LUCY REYNOLDS

In his study of America Jean Baudrillard famously recognised the compelling draw of the desert in Western culture. He noted how its blank grandeur reflected the aesthetics of '[T]he inhumanity of our ulterior, asocial, superficial world,'[1] offering in its sublime and inscrutable resistance to human agency, 'an ecstatic critique of culture, an ecstatic form of disappearance.'[2] Building on this persuasive notion of the desert as signifier for the barren conditions of late capitalism, Baudrillard observes the condition of its resistance to human intervention as: 'the luminous, fossilized network of an inhuman intelligence, of a radical indifference — the indifference not merely of the sky, but of the geological undulations, where the metaphysical passions of space and time alone crystallize.'[3]

The philosopher's description suggests that the desert functions as a space of temporal excess beyond the grasp and scale of human experience and measurement. The rocky sediment and strata which have shaped its arid landscapes allude to time spans of a planetary magnitude, which obliterate human comprehensions of temporality, rendering void our attempts at orientation through records of geological data, which ultimately become lost in the horizontal blankness of its endless plains of unimaginable time-scales. The desert's 'inhuman facticity',[4] produces, it might therefore be argued, a heightened, sensitised awareness of time, through our own inability to own it and grasp its dimensions. Its inhospitable expanse becomes instead a potent space of wish fulfilment, onto which imaginary narratives — national, cultural and individual — might be projected, and of which Baudrillard's vision of capitalism is but one.

It is not surprising that, as one of 20th century culture's most overt forms of wish fulfilment, the cinema should provide some of the most enduring and mythologised images of the desert through the genre of the American Western.[5] Read against the realities of political and social instabilities, the capitulation of the continent's last hostile regions to colonisation is imagined as a fiction of heroic and justified struggle. Peter Wollen, for example, highlights this delusion in relation to the films of the defining Western auteur director John Ford, where 'we see the celebration of a vast panorama of the American past. We see the American dream as it inspired immigrants and pioneers, the dream of an ideal moral community. But we also see the renunciation of the American present, the corruption of the

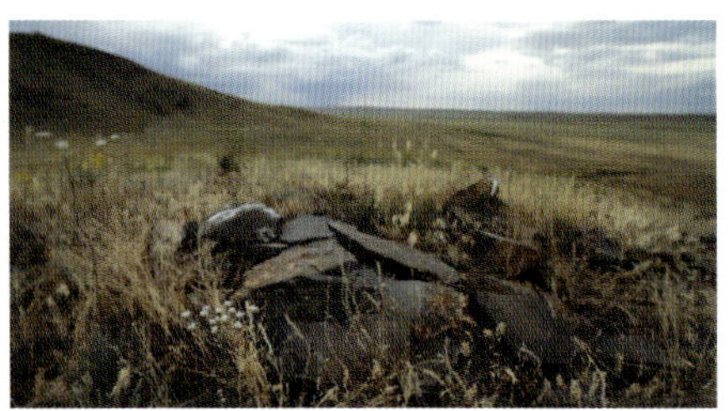

dream.' [6] The experience of overwhelming 'alien space', according to Yi-Fu
Tuan, inspired not only the pioneer dream of a civilised wilderness, but also
the potential for spiritual epiphany, as he notes: '...the loss of self in alien
space — even if it provides moments of ecstasy — means death. Explorers
of desert and ice may be said to be half in love with piercing beauty and
half in love with death.' [7] The writings of the Egyptian Desert Fathers, for
example, are some of the earliest, and most influential accounts of this lure
of the desert as a place to withdraw from society, finding in its inhospitable
spaces a spiritual succour derived from its very inability to sustain human
life.

Cinematic or spiritual, these human struggles to come to terms with
the overwhelming temporal/spatial dimensions, and implications, of the
desert are played out in Ruth Maclennan's film *Anarcadia*. But while the
desert of Baudrillard's eulogy, and Ford's idealism, is that arid terrain
redolent of American histories and myth making, her desert is the steppes
of south-eastern Kazakhstan, bordering China on the Asian fringe of
Russia, a place to which she has returned over several years to film. Like
Baudrillard's American desert, Kazakhstan's empty plains resonate with
a register of time tuned to unknowable, cosmic dimensions, just as its
featureless stretches resist the claims of territorial ownership: a blank
between borders. Maclennan's opening images situate the unnerving
grace of this unrelenting vastness in wide skies of scudding clouds, rocky
striations and grassy wastelands. Her film begins on the piebald neck of a
grazing horse, a reminder that the desert is hospitable to those creatures
whose demands on its resources are light and transitory.

Eschewing the grand vistas of the Western genre and the spectacular
landscape views of desert once pictured by photographers such as George
Muybridge or Ansel Adams, *Anarcadia*'s camera does not frame the
steppe at a distance. Instead, close-ups of grass, shard and shale reveal,
in shifting shades of tactile surface and texture, the nature that thrives in
these supposedly barren conditions. The steppe's immensities are depicted
not through the sweeping movement of a panning camera, the convention
most often associated with cinematic depictions of the desert. Instead
the natural dynamics of the desert found in the movements of wind, dust,
clouds and waving grass are framed through images of contemplative

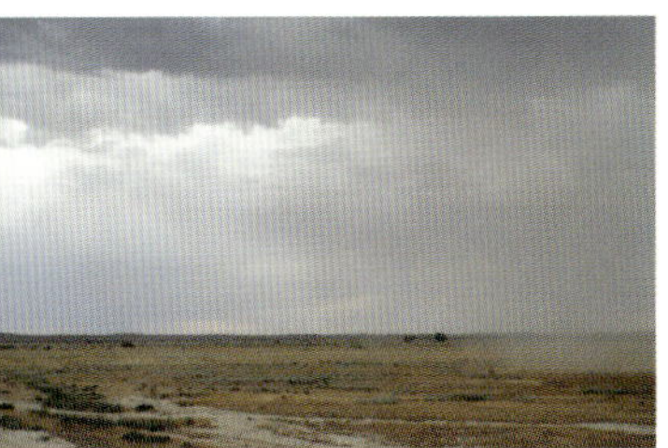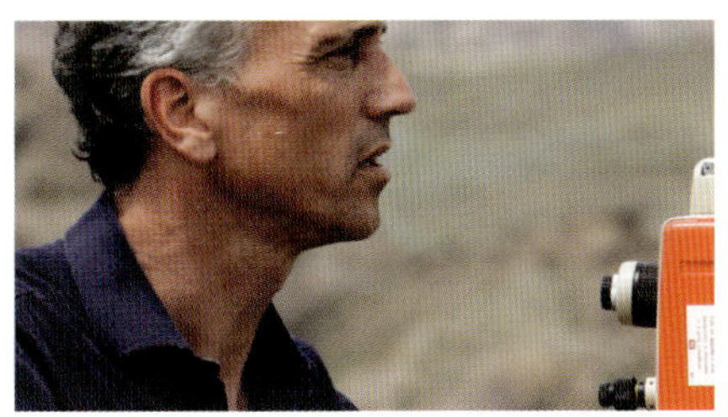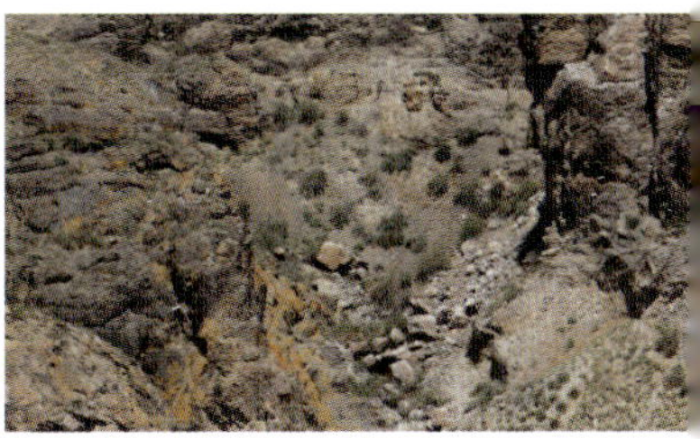

stillness or slow moving tracking shots. Sound is used sparingly, as birdsong and insect buzz are interposed with the music of Kuat Shildebaev, a Kazakh composer whose minimalist instrumentations of the Kazakh dombra, drum and jaw harp echo the spatial resonances of the desert landscape, as they evoke Eastern traditions of music-making.

To navigate the enigmas of this implacable landscape Maclennan invents two fictional guides: a prospector and an archaeologist, both struggling to extract meaning from the temporal inscriptions written into its rocky terrain. Both characters address the viewer rather than each other; their narratives are recounted in monologue, as confessions to the camera rather than exchange. Their paths do not converge but remain as separate tracks, framed by Maclennan's camera in their purposeful stride across the empty expanses of the desert, out of the frame and into nowhere. Perhaps this is because both follow, and exist in, different trajectories of time. The prospector looks ahead to opportunity, reading potential for wealth in the desert's time-pocked surfaces, speaking a litany of geological riches: 'cyclocarbons, mono-olefins, and alkenes'. His kinship to the itinerant pan-handlers and chancers of the Western is underscored by mention of Tombstone and tumbleweed. However, he refers beyond cinematic archetype to the on-going narratives of mineral exploration, speculation and extraction that from Brazil to Sierra Leone, scatter the globe. Literalised in his equipment, the prospector's gaze is towards the future as he maps out the landscape through the long-range viewfinder of a geological surveyor's tool known as a theodolyte. Maclennan's camera eye follows his, focusing in on the patterns of lichen and striated contours of rocky erosion, in which he envisages mineral wealth.

The archaeologist, by contrast, searches for traces of the past in the rubble around her feet, pacing sedimented banks, not of ancient strata, but the detritus of more recent human habitation. Unlike the prospector her features, and soft cadences of speech, reveal her Kazakh, possibly local, origins. Framed close to the ground, against the red earth, she reads the desert not as a wide vista, but as a shifting surface of loose earth and rubble which may divulge secrets. For despite her fictional characterisation, the archaeologist delineates the collapsed contours of a historical reality, a compelling narrative of counterpoint to the American

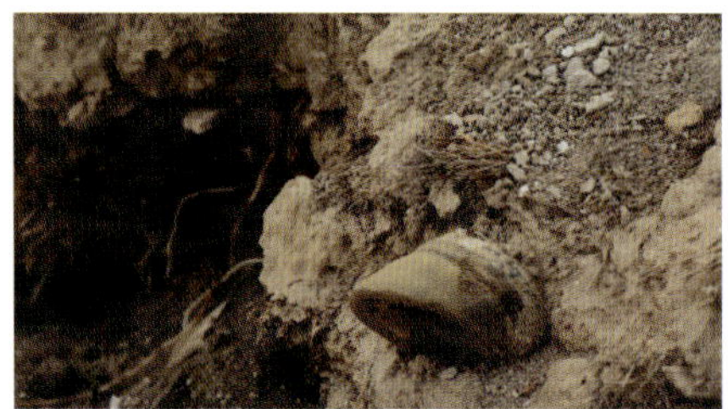 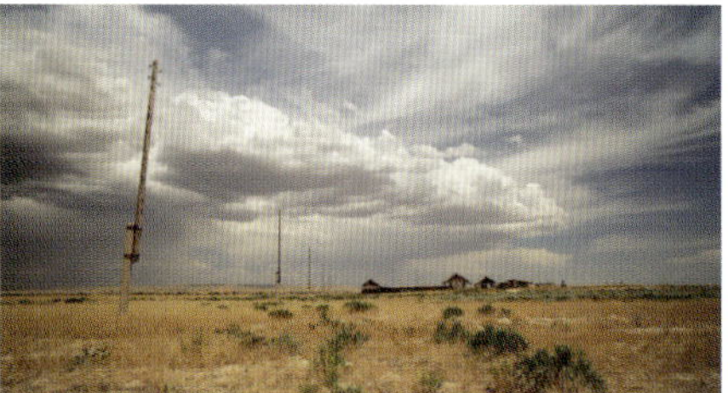

West, which drew Maclennan to this forsaken place. Mirroring the territorial ambitions of its capitalist rival, the Turkestan-Siberian railway, or 'Turk-Sib,' was built across the steppes, pressing teams of workers into service, many from the labour camps that dotted the area, to lay it mile upon mile. One of the most acclaimed and defining depictions of the Turk-Sib railway project is woven together in the celebratory montage of Victor Turin's documentary film *Turk-Sib* (1929). Echoing the imaginings of Maclennan's fictional prospector, the desert is presented as a space of activity and opportunity, where valuable oil and minerals could be tapped, where factories could be built and power lines erected.

This Soviet documentary, like the Western, depicts the civilising of the wilderness as a moral imperative, but where it diverges from its American counterpart is in its ideological emphasis, stressing a pioneer dream of Communist collectivism, materialised in the assimilative suture of Soviet montage, rather than the narrative of the rugged outsider and the pioneer communities of the American Western. A notably exultant image of the capitulation of the desert, embodied in the Kazakh tribesmen as well as the landscape, is represented in its exhilarating use of montage. As a train gathers steam through slowly accelerating cuts between tracks and turning wheels, a group of ethnic horseman first look on and then race joyfully against the speeding train. The tracks across the desert represent the Eden of modern progress, a technological sublime of speeding train, in answer to, and in competition with, the spatial magnitudes of desert expanse. The tribesmen's futile chase infers that although human technology has subjugated the power of the desert, its inhabitants accept its changes: running alongside, they will not be left behind.

For in order to fully defeat the desert, the sublime experience engendered by its immensities, as Turin's film proves, is met and challenged by the alternative 'inhuman facticity' of the train's own sublime of technological spectacle, inspiring the awe of speed in racing tribesmen, just as it had once enthralled European cinema audiences at the turn of the century. The simultaneous contrast and convergence between the train and the Kazakh tribespeople set up in Turin's use of montage emphasises the necessary absorption of the pre-technological into the modernist mechanics of the Soviet era. In another telling image, a camel bends to examine the tracks in

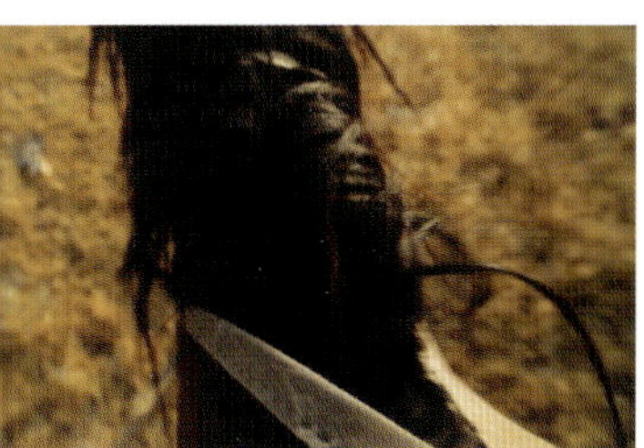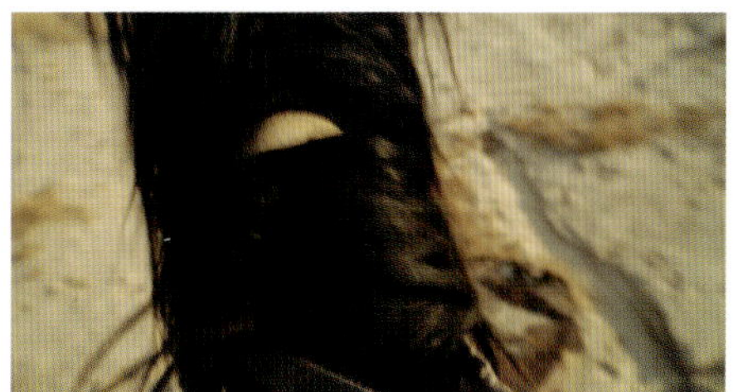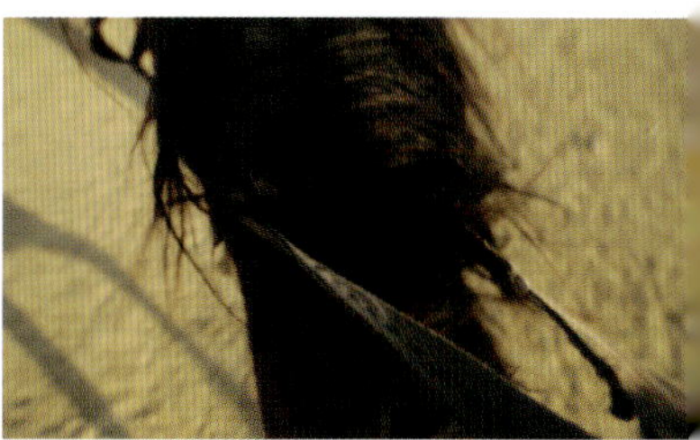

the desert, as one mode of transport is superseded by another. Maclennan's film, on the other hand, resonates with the absence of this conquering technology, now routed by the desert and the erosions of history. Yet, the air of melancholy and loss which could pervade *Anarcadia* is lifted by passages of joyful momentum to equal Turin's. Framed behind the tufted mane of a desert horse, for example, the camera makes an exhilarating, jolting journey across the steppe, rhythmically counterpointed by drumbeat and the intonations of the archaeologist's musing voice, as she considers past desert dwellers lost in prehistory: 'did people start by writing stories or riding horses?'

Yet, it could be argued that the desert prevails over all human attempts to reach for the sublime. The expression of eternity evoked in its receding prairies and rocky castellations exposes the ideological oppositions of the 20th century as mere skirmishes on the edges of a time span profoundly indifferent to history and human memory, which flattens their chronologies into the featureless horizons of its plains. The futility of human attempts to penetrate and leave their mark upon the desert could be seen as the central concern of Maclennan's film, poignantly manifesting in the steppes, ruins and fruitless searches of *Anarcadia's* protagonists. For, where the archaeologist now paces a station house once stood optimistically pre-empting the promise of the train's arrival. But the railway never came, along with the rumour that this remote site was destined to become the new capital of Kazakhstan, finally abandoned in favour of train-tracks passing further East. All that remains of the station house are the bricks upon which the archaeologist crouches. Built by forced labour from nearby gulags between 1929 and 1933, according to neighbours' accounts, the eroded walls of the lost station house inevitably function as a resonant metaphor for the demise of communism, now dissolved into the unrelenting desert of capitalism recognised by Baudrillard. This remnant of Soviet presence has attained the 'ecstatic form of disappearance' observed by Baudrillard; its scant remains sink back into the stony matter of the desert, like a skeleton picked clean and now indistinguishable from the fossilised rubble of earlier millennia.

Processes of erasure and sublimation are also addressed in *Capital*, a companion piece to *Anarcadia,* in which contemporary footage of a

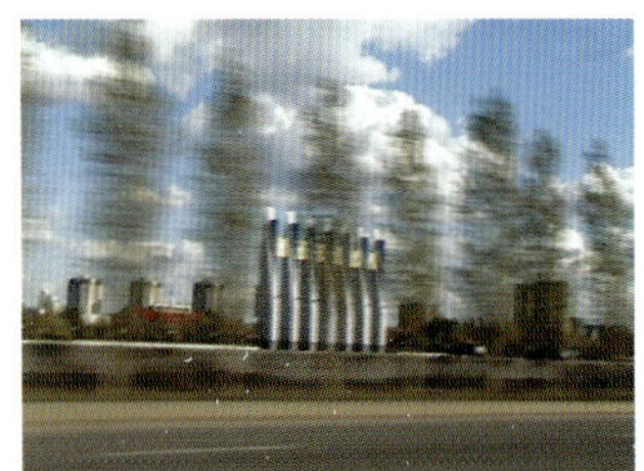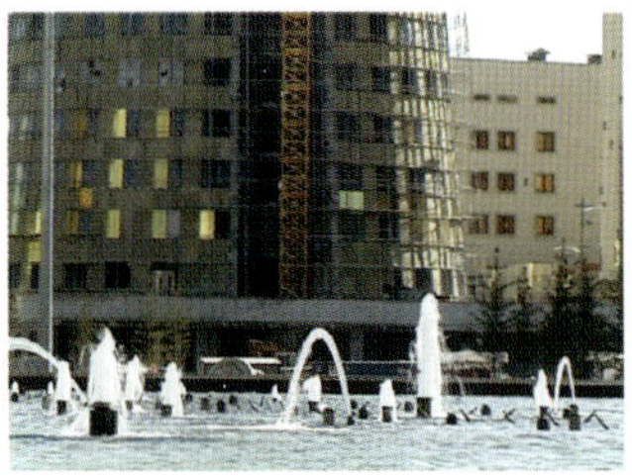

present-day Kazakh city is again navigated through the device of fiction.
The viewer surveys this unnamed city with the guidance of an imaginary
traveller, who is reporting on its customs and architecture to a royal ruler,
in whose honour, it is implied, the city has been rebuilt. Through this
allegorical structure, which has the tone and address of a child's fable,
Maclennan confronts the relentless building programmes which have
characterised post-Soviet Kazakhstan. Just as the technological sublime
of the railway at the beginning of the century had sought to conquer the
magnitude of the desert, so the dazzling towers of the ruler's new kingdom
embody a new economic regime, through a spectacle of awe, and inhuman
proportions, which asserts one iteration of modernisation over the last,
in a ceaseless roll of erasures driven by ideology, whether of collectivism
or commerce. As Marc Augé has argued, 'architecture does transmit in
a sense the illusions of the current dominant ideology and plays a part
in the aesthetic of transparency and reflection, height and harmony, the
aesthetic of distance which, deliberately or not, supports those illusions
and expresses the triumph of the system…' [8] Augé's observations are
both literally and metaphorically borne out in the glass-clad high rises
and fountains pictured in *Capital*, whose faceted surfaces, like fairground
halls of mirrors, reflect back an evasive spectacle of distortion and
fragmentation, exerting a form of obfuscatory deflection in which, as
Maclennan's off-screen traveller observes to her ruler: 'I cannot see my
own reflection, but I can see you everywhere I look.'

The shimmering lack of substance conjured by the buildings in *Capital*
might be seen as a materialised mirage of the 'ulterior, asocial, superficial
world' once conjured by Baudrillard from the desert's blankness. [9] In
this city designed for 'dream-settlers', as *Capital*'s narrator informs us:
'most streets are not yet real. They are works in progress drawn in the
dirt, passable, but indistinct and unmappable.' Not yet built, yet built
on a city that already exists, *Capital* depicts a space suspended in an
indeterminate temporality. The narrator's placatory address to her prince
locates her visit in the ageless 'once upon a time' of fables, redolent of
collective aural memory, while the architecture of the new city orientates
us towards a utopian future. In this temporal oscillation between past
and future, the experience of the present, as Augé notes, manifests as:
'…a lack that structures the present moment by orientating it towards the

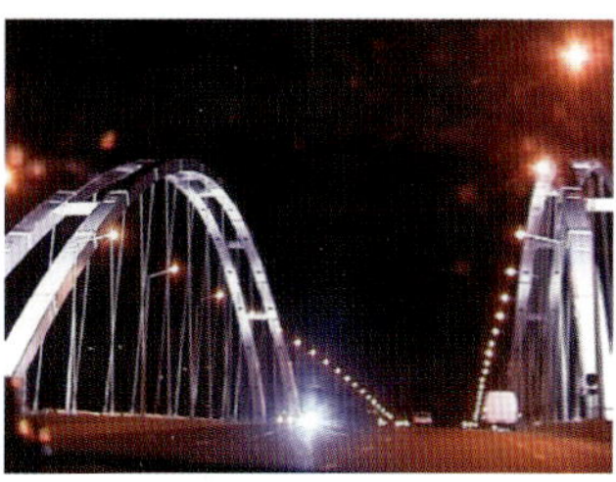

past or the future. It arises equally well from the sight of the Acropolis or of the Guggenheim Museum in Bilbao.'[10] The lack of material present that Augé delineates, it could be argued, subject to the allusions of the past's relics and the future's projections, engenders a temporal disorientation similar to that experienced in the extinguishing magnitudes of desert. To address this pervading sense of loss and restore balance, the archaeologist might imagine a vanished narrative of the ideal civic community: a 'dream city' of 'kitchen gardens and washing machines'; or the settler of the Prince's perfect city might find, as the narrator puts it 'pride, adventure, consumption, wealth'. Both are imaginary projections, which grapple, as I have discussed, with the sublime and incomprehensible 'inhuman facticity' shared by the desert and human progress.

Capital also alludes to a condition of vertical disappearance, as one vision of the present is built upon another. Functioning like a form of urban palimpsest, *Capital*'s narrator observes, a now invisible race of 'pre-dreamers' exists in the hidden city: 'They move through the spaces where the capital is rising up, but they inhabit another city, one that no longer exists except in traces, smudges from the past.'
The vanished city of 'pre-dreamers' recalls the 'out-moded' Parisienne arcades of the 19th century, 'residues of a dream-world' [11] which Walter Benjamin and the Surrealists saw as symptomatic of industrialised culture. Significantly, Benjamin's notion of the 'out-moded' refers to the ruins of recent obsolescence: 'what emerges from these wish images is the resolute effort to distance oneself from all that is antiquated — which includes, however, the recent past. [12] These tendencies deflect the imagination (which is given impetus by the new) back upon the primal past.' Thus, the erased city which *Capital* frames, still discernible in pavements that peter out, and the melancholy of faded signs and boarded up buildings, adopt the proportions and patina of the mythic, a Benjaminian 'Ur-history', [13] which the narrator discerns as 'a lost world [is] retained in hieroglyphics of rusted playgrounds.'

What Benjamin does not touch on, but Hal Foster would later elaborate, is the uncanny aspect that circulates within these structures erased by progress. This is the spectral presence of an urban population who, as Maclennan's allegory infers, have become the outmoded of the new East.

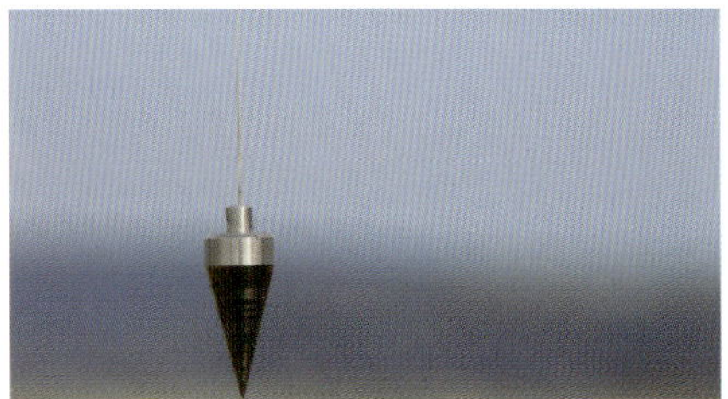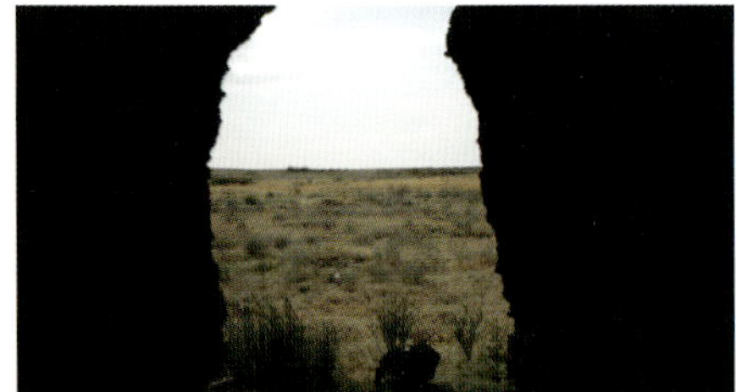

Referring to the Freudian notion of the uncanny, where, 'once repressed, the past, however blessed, cannot return so benignly,' [14] Foster sees the 'out-moded' assume a 'demonic guise' for the Surrealists, so that Louis Aragon could exclaim that: 'the old arcade is full of "sirens", "sphinxes", and other ciphers of desire and death.' [15] It could be argued that a similar haunting is evident in *Capital*, where the narrator glimpses the 'invisible people' who inhabit the spectral city crushed beneath the new, and whose resonant absence populates the empty parks, playgrounds and half-built streets.

Benjamin and Augé, as well as *Capital*'s insistent narrator, remind us of the illusory tricks played by these compelling spaces, conjuring projections of lost and future utopias from urban and natural desert alike. Indeed, the archaeologist's attempt to grasp the histories of the steppes could be seen to echo those of the filmmaker, whose own pilgrimage to this inaccessible region of the steppe was based on an unsubstantiated story of a lost station-house, recounted to her on a previous visit to Kazakhstan. In this way, Maclennan rehearses the same gestures of recovery as her fictional characters, prospecting in the desert on the promise of an overlooked seam of the past which may illuminate some aspect of Kazakhstan's buried histories. Like desert travellers before her, it could be argued that the lost station house is a mirage, a search for 'fools gold'.

However, film is an ideal medium for navigating the desert. Its spectral projections can withstand the rigours of desert conditions, peopling the desert with human presence at no risk to life, building imagined town and communities which place little demand on the desert's scant resources. Made of light and air, its celluloid communities do not suffer the desert's unforgiving erasures; as mirages themselves, they are subject to their own acts of dematerialisation, and have the power of repeat appearance, their former dimensions intact and immune to its environmental ravages. Like the desert, the moving image is also a crystalline expression of time and space, [16] albeit on a scale addressed to human histories. Film's material expression of passing time infuses cinema with the heightened perception of time-past, of death and loss which also resonates in the desert's harsh yet sublime conditions, and resurfaces in the invisible city hidden within the capital, like the uncanny outmoded which first haunted

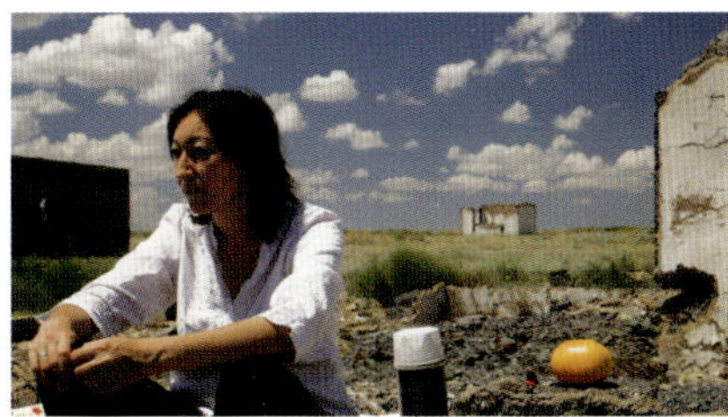 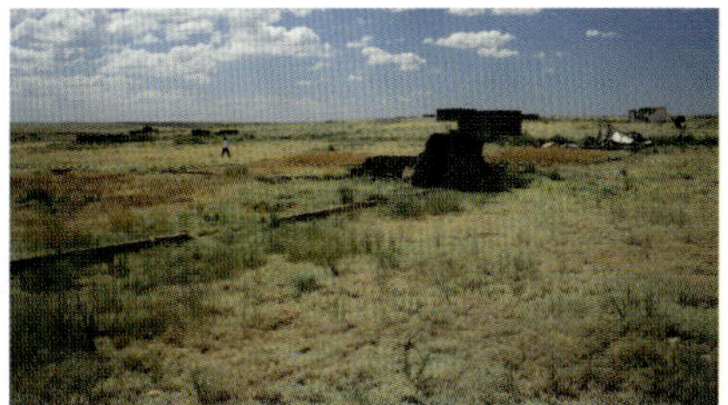

the Surrealists. *Anarcadia* and *Capital*'s convergences of fact and fictions, material presence and absent histories, reflect these unlikely kinships and juxtapositions at the same time as they cast doubt upon them. Speaking of the desert, Maclennan stresses that it is 'not just a vista to be panned over.' Her assertion refers not only to the dynamic ecologies which its harsh conditions support, and her images frame, or the temporal/spatial sublime which has struck awe into countless travellers, on the page and on the screen. For the fictional voices of archaeologist, prospector and visiting dignitary weave narratives not just for the tragedies of Kazakhstan's lost and contested territories, but also for the melancholy of a modern condition, where political and economic expediencies have created, as Baudrillard has suggested, and Maclennan's films attest, a desert of human design.

1 Baudrillard, Jean, *America*, Verso, New York, London, 1988, p5
2 Ibid
3 Ibid p6
4 Ibid
5 The film genre developed from a long tradition of western frontier literature, beginning with the nineteenth century adventure stories of James Fenimore Cooper, such as *The Prairie* (1824), and expanding into a popular genre of comic, film, television serials and dime novels. For further details see: Lyon, Thomas J, *The Literary West: An Anthology of Western American Literature*, Oxford University Press, New York, 1999.
6 Wollen, Peter, 'John Ford', *New Left Review* no 29, Jan/Feb 1965, reprinted in Caughie, John, (ed) *Theories of Authorship*, Routledge/BFI, London, 1981 p102
7 Ibid p155
8 Augé, Marc, *Non-Places: An Introduction to Supermodernity*, Verso, London, 1998, pXVI
9 Baudrillard, Jean, *America*, Verso, New York, London, 1988, p5
10 Ibid
11 Benjamin, Walter, (1935) 'Paris the Capital of the Nineteenth Century, Jennings, Michael (ed) *Writer of Modern Life; Essays on Charles Baudelaire*, Belknap Press of Harvard University Press, Cambridge Massachusetts, 2006 p45
12 Ibid p32
13 See Buck-Morss, Susan, *The Dialectics of Seeing: Walter Benjamin and the Arcades Project*, MIT Press, Cambridge, Massachusetts, 1989, for a fuller elucidation of this notion.
14 Foster, Hal, *Compulsive Beauty*, MIT Press, Cambridge, Massachusetts, 1993 p164
15 Ibid
16 See Deleuze, Gilles, *Cinema 2*, Athlone Press, London, 1989, p68-97 for his study of this principle.

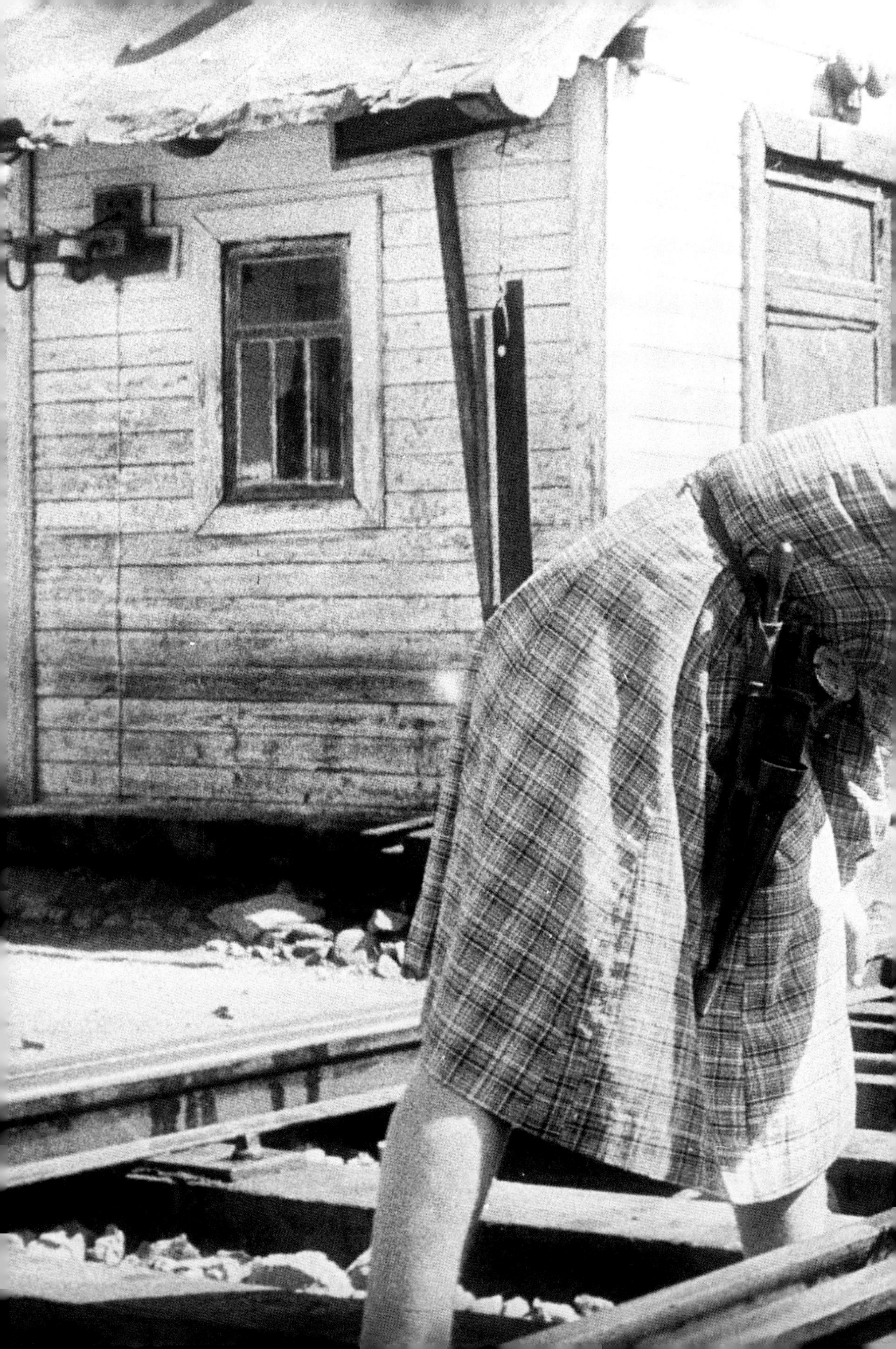

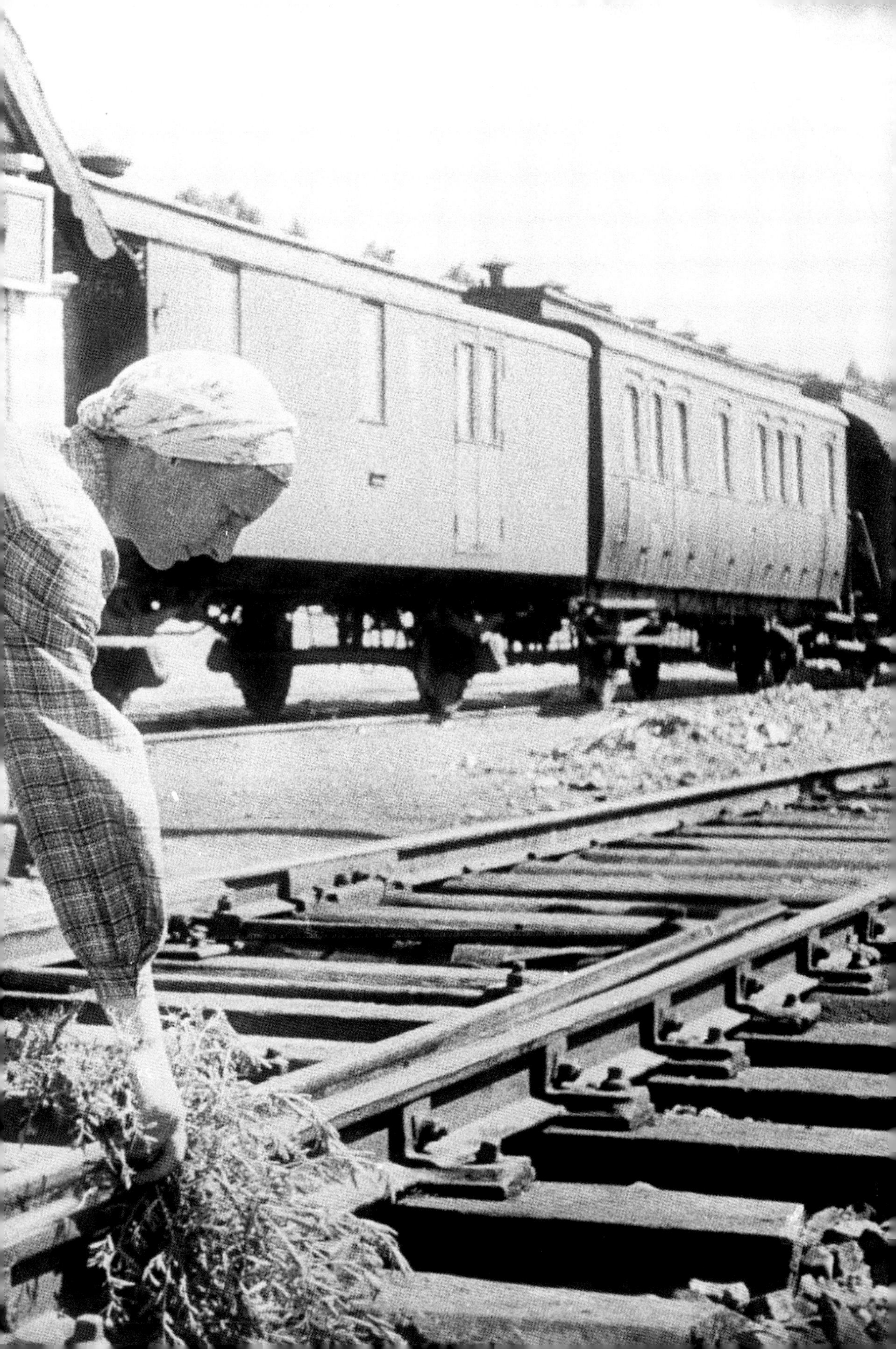

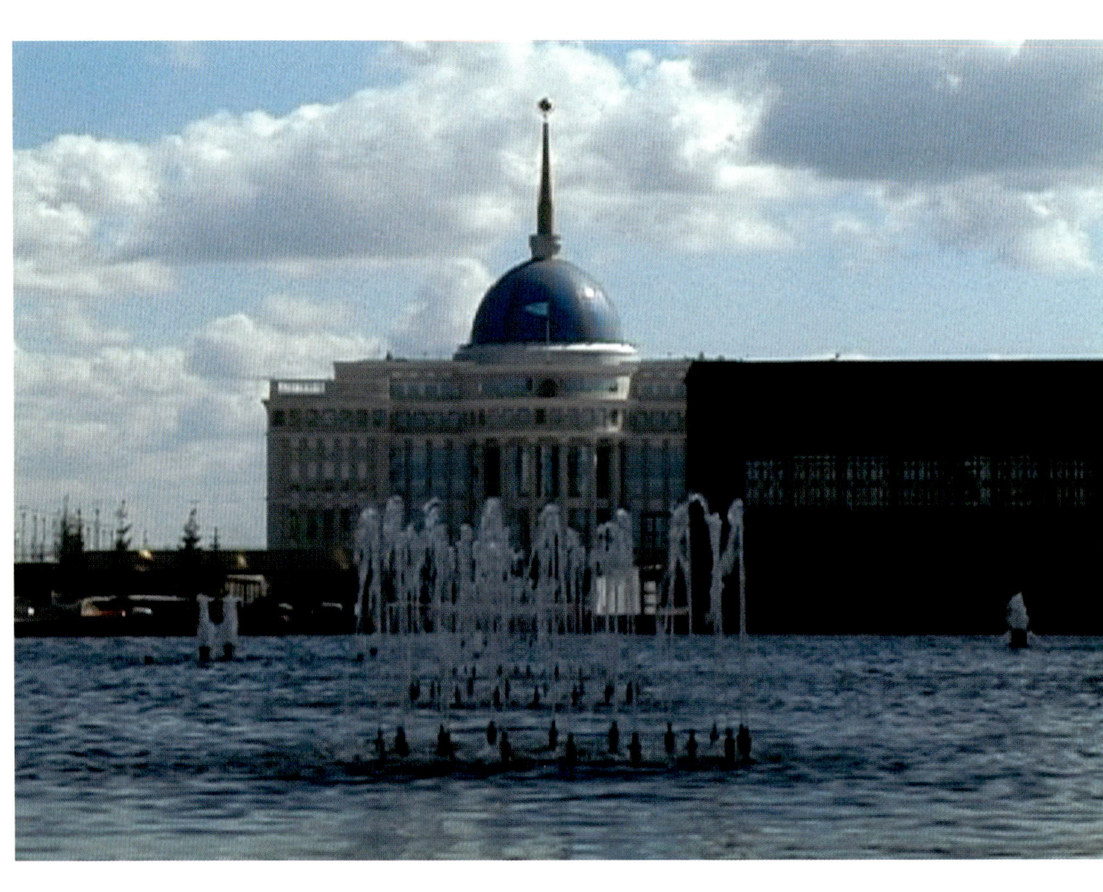

SCREENPLAY

Prince,
I've come to the capital from far away, beyond the desert, beyond the mountains, beyond the Western sea. I have travelled for weeks and days and hours. The city is a whirl of traffic, rumours, and black dust. I cannot see my own reflection but I can see you everywhere I look.

Do the fountains make you feel safe, Prince?
Fountains cheer people up, you say. Everyone loves a fountain — it helps

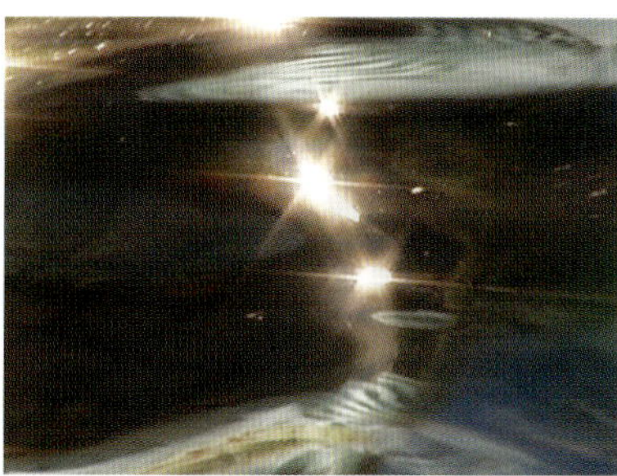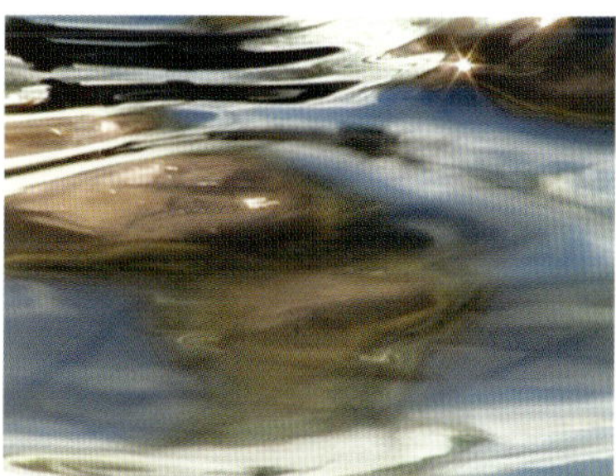

them to forget their worries. Helps them to forget... I'm told there is a fountain where the orphanage used to stand, a domino fountain instead of the old House of Toys, and a fountain with a leaping horse instead of the old chess club. A pond is being dug where the over-forties disco was held, once a month, on a Tuesday.

You have designed public space to distract revolutionaries. Fountains block the way to the Parliament, to your palace and to the courthouse. Dutiful subjects feed the pigeons. The fountains are equipped with 3D cameras, facial recognition and simulation decoders, heat and movement sensors and all hidden biometric devices. Nothing goes unnoticed. Except...the city itself. The State archive is a giant inlaid egg, the contents destroyed or moved — no one knows which. The parliament is actually a theatre; the theatre the courthouse; the courthouse a casino. The casino is...a place of worship.

The revolutions have already taken place: the martyrs have been honoured, the victims forgotten. The capital is thousands of miles from any other city or hostile neighbour. Everything is safe. And in fact all areas that seem

public are owned by a private consortium, chaired by your son-in-law. These
are divided into zones, guarded by dogs and private security guards. You
also have your own personal elite mounted guard.

Prince,
Sand blows continuously through the parks. These give people room to
breathe. But there are no gardeners. No one knows the names of any trees.
All the plants have been imported from a distant island. And they're dying,
so gardeners are being imported too. Lawns are difficult to grow, but the
elite must play golf.

Prince,
I hear you have generously donated a new sports arena to your subjects,
so that they may enjoy 'state of the art sporting facilities in a specially
landscaped park'. It is adorned with works by eminent artists, inspired by
the national culture and heritage. A plastic imitation bronze Zoroastrian
pissoir is planted in the middle of a bed of tulips.

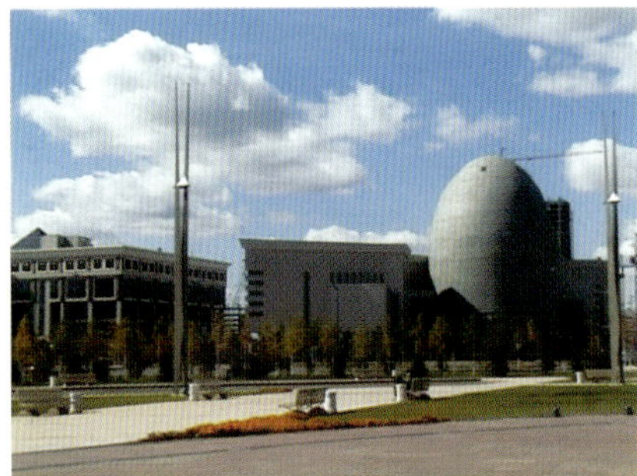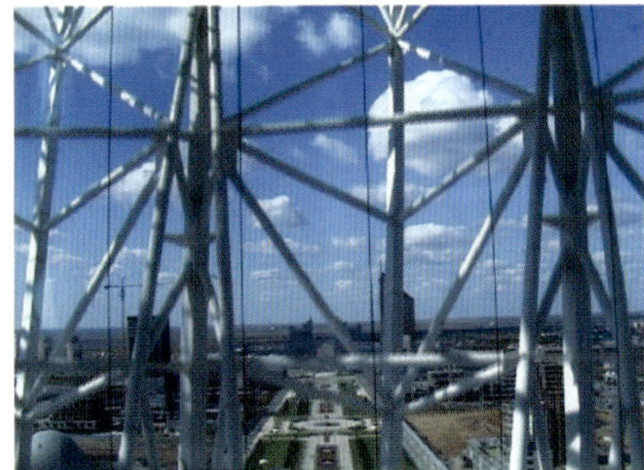

But the wind is ferocious. Windsocks are replaced daily. The thousands of
flags you ordered are all shredded. The inhabitants no longer hear the wind,
and have learned to speak in the pauses between roars.

I am puzzled Prince,
Why have you erected so many monuments in this unborn capital? You like to
remind people of who they are. Yes, strange... I have seen statues of hooded
eagles, ravaged horses, wingless doves, burnt wheat sheaves, dead fish.

One troubling habit I notice: no one ever turns to look at me. They look away.

Prince,
Will this city ever be real?

I learned something new today, Prince.
As you know, a foreign architect designed the capital. You may not know,
however, that there are another two versions. All three plans are being laid

out at the same time, and whichever plan is finished first and pleases you, Prince, will be built in concrete, faced with mirrors. In the meantime, the capital is a potential city, a partial city of crossed lines and multiple street names. People live in whichever version has been chosen for them. Doctors, lawyers, teachers, actors, and joiners, all follow the foreign architect's plan. The ministers and deputies, maître d's, waiters, chauffeurs, chemists, car dealers, bankers and croupiers, follow another plan, the runner up in your competition. The shopkeepers, farmers, greengrocers, children, hairdressers, pensioners, nurses, and artists, follow the plan of the old city, which has been torn down, but was hurriedly reinstated when it was learnt that you were interested in rediscovering your country's heritage. That plan has now been abandoned but not everyone realises it. Some people still live in it, trying to recall what was there, and what has been rebuilt, and what is part of a new plan.

Throughout the city, winds blast through the empty rooms of unfinished high-rise dolls' houses, dispersing dreams and dust. At the weekend city dwellers flee, swept along empty streets like dead leaves. This morning

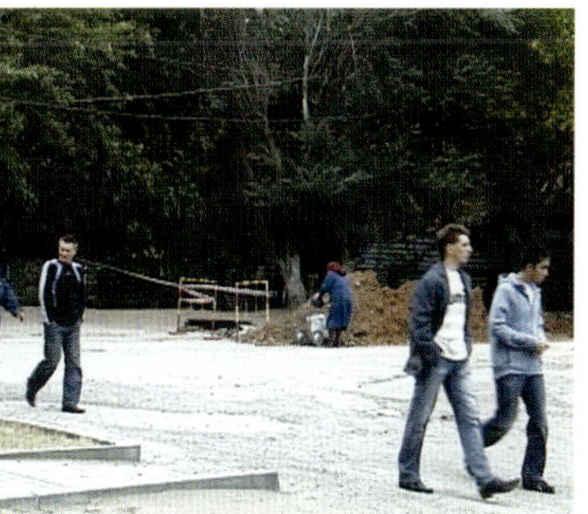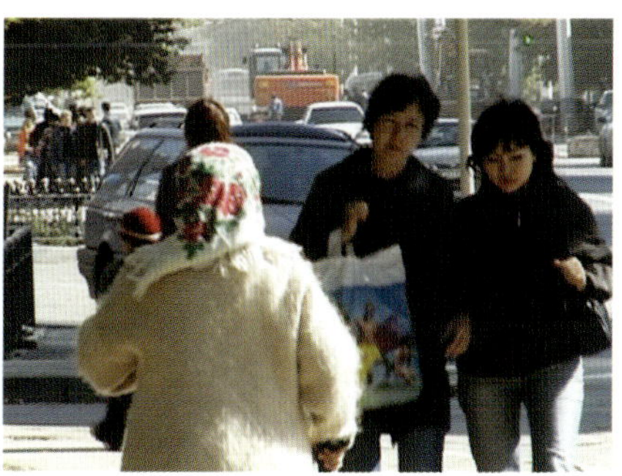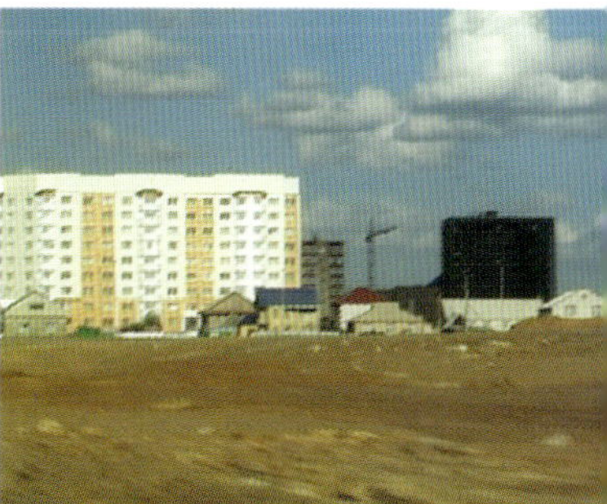

as I walked along one of the capital's vast avenues and turned a corner, following instructions, looking for a shop to buy a loaf of bread and a chicken, the street disintegrated. A billboard promised new homes in dream developments, 'Talisman', 'Edelweiss', 'Millenium'... But I kept walking in circles, in the dirt, tripping over pavements that were either too high, or non-existent.

Prince,
Do you know that a woman, Kara, who gave birth to a son, Genghiz, who drowned in the river, lived in a hut on what is now a traffic island in the middle of a roundabout? I saw her visiting the roundabout, to bury a rock. I later met Ivan who lived nearby in a hut with a vegetable plot, given to him for good behaviour at the factory. The plot is now a fountain that plays 'Jingle Bells' and 'Yesterday'. He told me that one of the imported pigeons drowned in it last week, from eating too much marzipan.
There is no fresh fruit anymore. It is all flown in, just enough to feed the rich.

Yesterday, I saw an old woman walk through a parking lot, carrying a bag
of potatoes and light-bulbs. She walked straight through the railings, and
the apartment block wall — the one next to the pharmacy on what was Well
Street (the new name, 'Victory Boulevard' is stencilled on the corner, but the
old sign still hangs above it). The lady disappeared from view as I crossed
the road to ask for directions. She is a seamstress, I was told, who works
nights sewing sequins on ballet dresses for your court troupe.

And minutes ago, Prince, I met a woman, Gul, who designs interiors for your
city's wealthy immigrants. I hear there's an endless flow of clients. She's
good at helping save the rich from their own bad taste... and of course at
spending enough money... Revenues here are good. The capital is a Free
Economic Zone.

Prince,
All I hear in the capital is good news. Nothing nasty ever happens in this
city, it seems. And fortunately, if it does, it's forgotten almost instantly. It
disappears like smoke, leaving no trace, except perhaps a dusting of yellow ash.

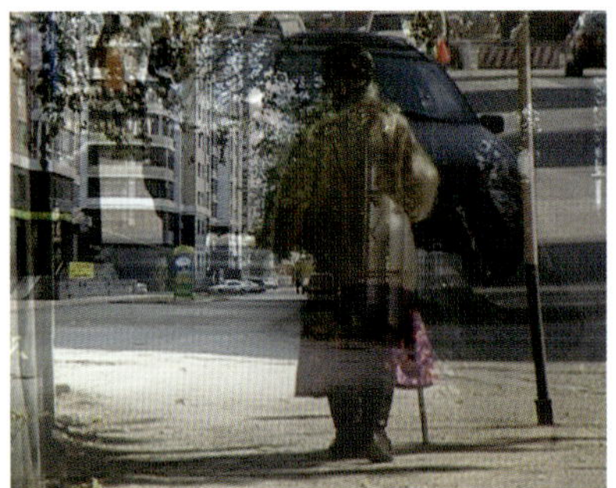
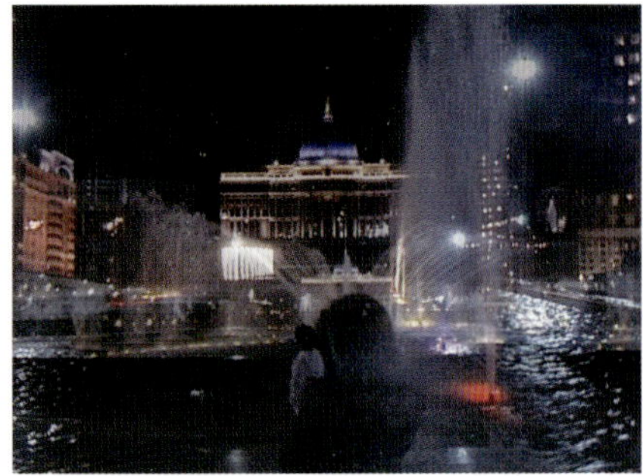

Money spurts out of the ground, exploding from the cracked earth. It
circulates from shiny suit pocket, to envelope, to plastic card, to numbers,
to letterheads, then out into the open: black lace evening gowns, silver fox
fur, diamonds, black pearls, black cars, black suits, black ties. Money flows
on ballet, gambling, VIP lounge service, champagne, on dazzling lawns with
private pools and deadly dogs with deadly stares... Everything is light light
light: all light and spinning casino wheels, and flashing smiles, and white
teeth, shiny rings, shiny tans, shiny cars, and shiny...furs.

Prince,
Your capital is for dreamers. And it has room for many more dreamers,
attracted by promises of wealth, power and influence. Free money, fast
power, free influence, from hand to hand, mouth to mouth, circulating,
expanding, swallowing everything. Exhilarating. Windy, youthful, empty.

No one is forced to dream your dream, you say. But why would they not want
to? What else could they possibly want?

People say they believe in your dream capital; they say it's beautiful; but no one seems to love it. No one will die to save it or anything it harbours.

The city is like a child who is not loved for himself, but for what he might do one day; or a woman who has been bought and silenced, made to change her name, her clothes, her face.

No one loves the capital's cracks and dirt. No one is allowed to notice them. Love requires people to accept a past lived without them. Love requires appreciation of the mind, body, flesh, blood, and waste. Many people fear and hate this city but have too much to lose; so all they can do is whisper between the lines.

Doubt is forbidden; doubt is dangerous. Pride, adventure, consumption, wealth — so much is at stake in the laminated capital.

So much is being spent by the administration, by foreign investors, settlers, diplomats, even the cowboys — so belief is paramount.

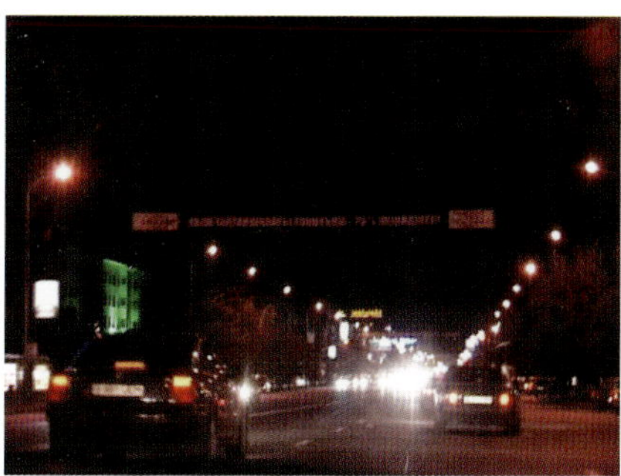
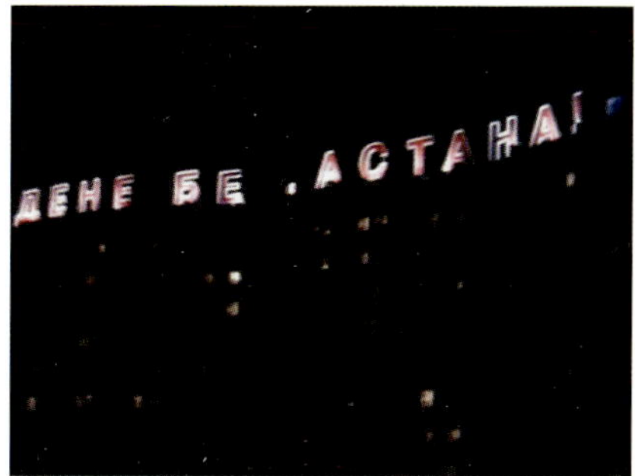

But, Prince,
You should look out for the people who are not living in your dream.

I see a city of parallel dreams. They intersect in the street, or rather what passes for a street. Most streets are not yet real. They are works in progress drawn in the dirt, passable, but indistinct and unmappable.

The recently landed dream-settlers never speak to the pre-dreamers.

The pre-dreamers exist alongside the life of the capital. They were here before, but are now invisible. They move through the spaces where the capital is rising up, but they inhabit another city, one that no longer exists except in traces, smudges from the past.

Little heaps of sunflower seed husks appear where people used to wait for buses, or for children after school.

A lost world is retained in hieroglyphics of rusted playgrounds scattered through the city, their bright primary colours rubbed to subtle shades that speak of experience. These remains are stranded until a plan can be carried out to dispose of them and use the space for something more...expensive.

Prince,
On my way to the capital I met an old hermit who warned me to leave the city after three days. He said the capital would fulfil all my dreams, and yet bring me nothing.

'This is a strange kind of city,' I said. I now understand what he meant. The life that feeds the city's dream has all but disappeared. Experience is missing. Instead, colourful, hybrid rites are being invented and performed, injected with memories of a culture that never existed.

'Soon a terrible plague will descend on the city,' warned the hermit.

'The mirrors and fountains will reflect nothing except the prince. People

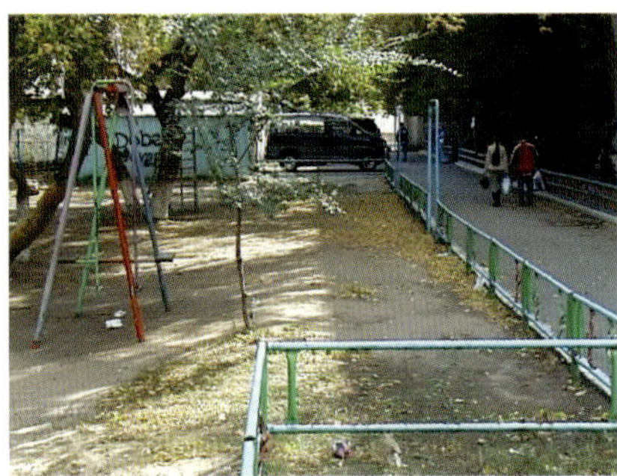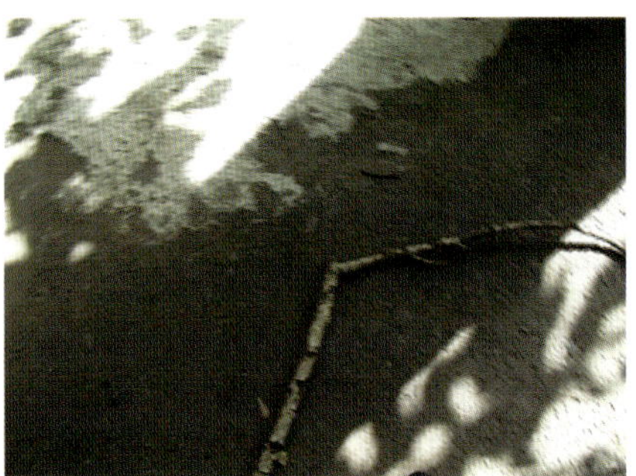

will all dream the same dream. There will be no escape from it, no memories left. No language to speak of anything old, or anything new, nothing left to remember, nothing even to forget.'

Beware.

I must leave your palace now, Prince. May I take a piece of this city with me — a shard of broken glass from your mirror?

I shall tell the tale of this city in my own land. Tell me, what should I say?

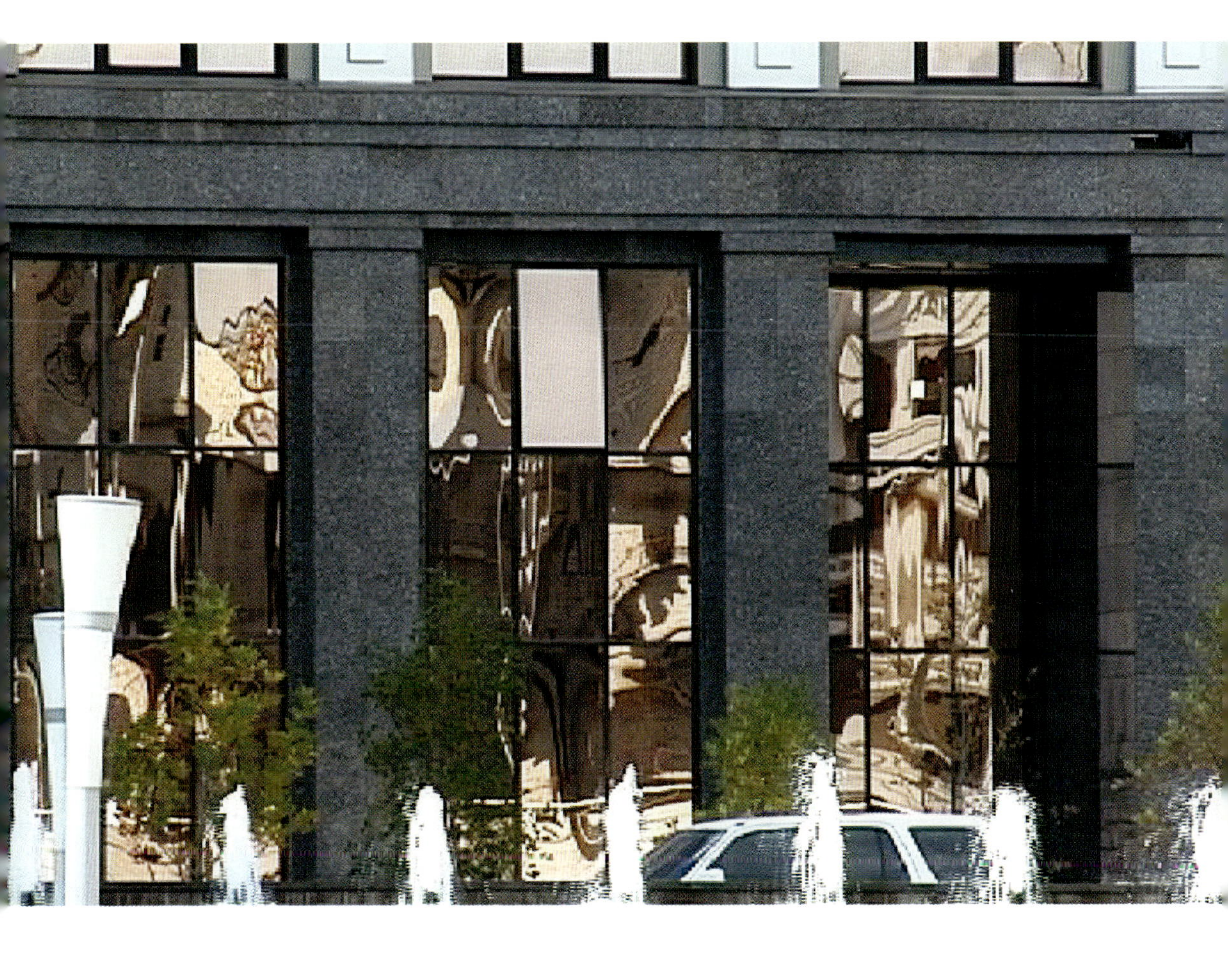

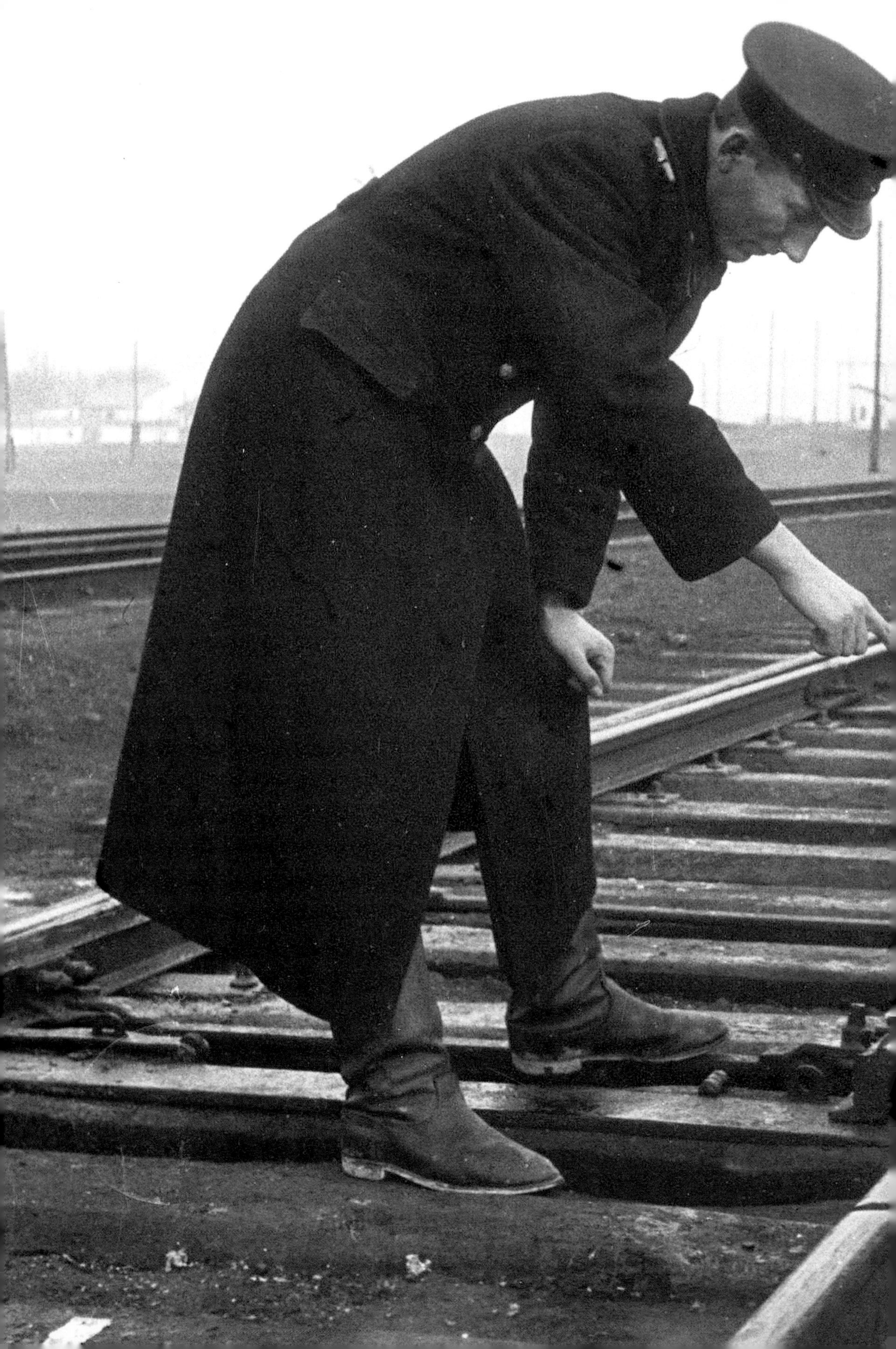

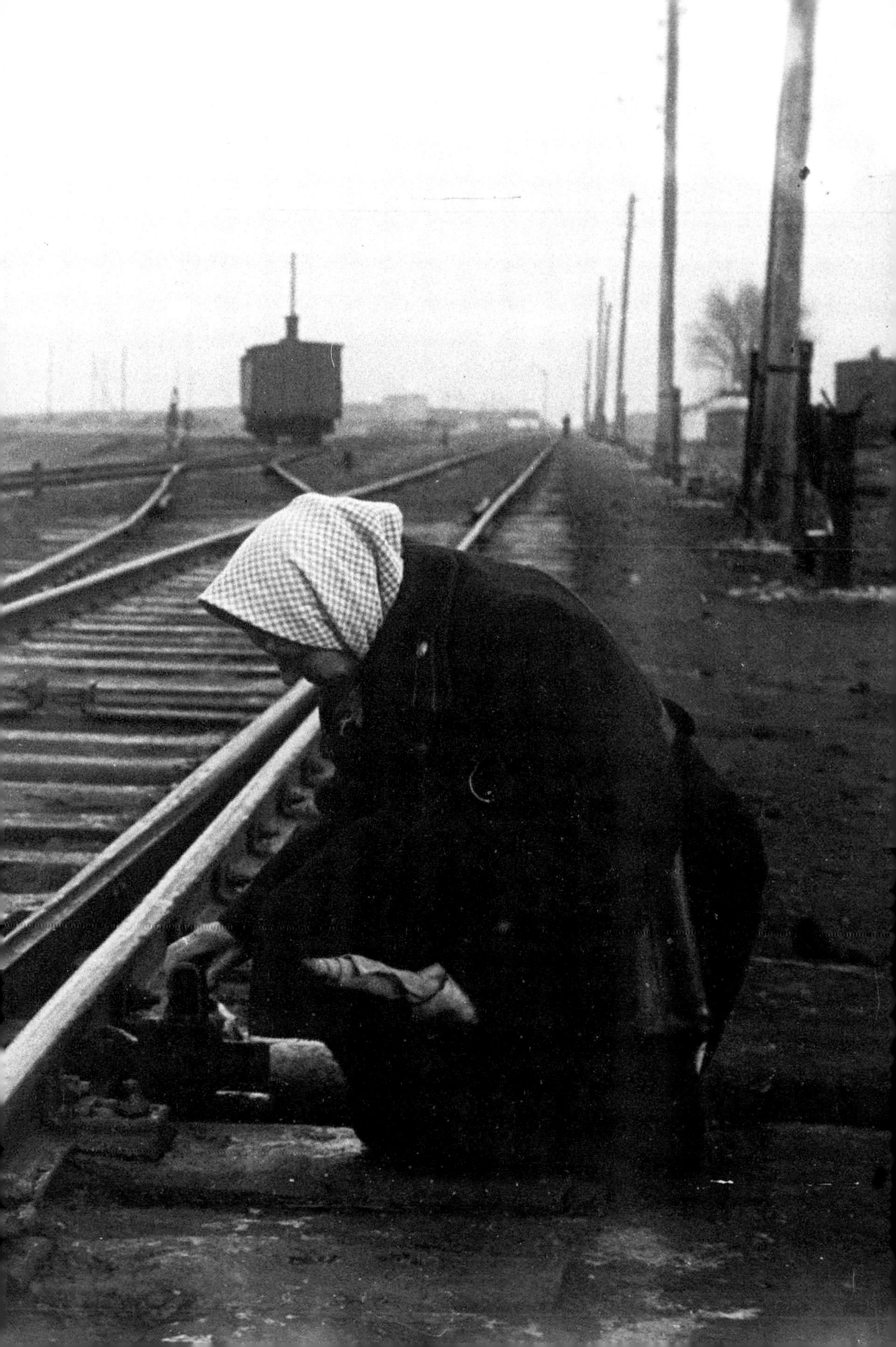

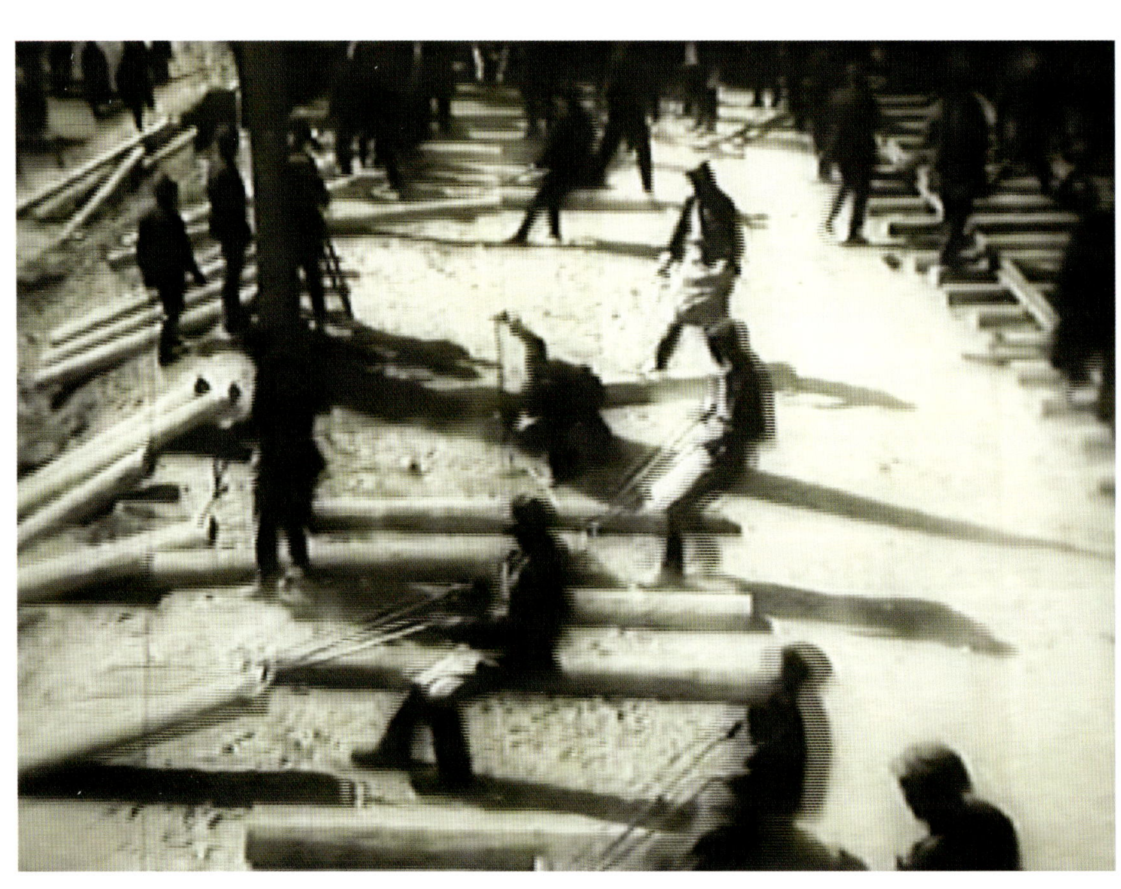

John Hansard Gallery, Southampton
Thursday 9 December, 2010

OH: I'll start with asking what attracted you to the post-Soviet countries, to Kazakhstan in particular, and to the two places in the films in the exhibition — Astana and the much more indefinable area in *Anarcadia*.

RM: I studied Russian at university and then lived in Moscow for a year in 1989/1990. At the time it was still the Soviet Union, but it was rapidly unravelling. In fact it unravelled completely while I was there[1]. I was chatting to a curator, Anna Harding, in 2005 who had been to Kazakhstan at the invitation of the British Council and had met young curators of contemporary art there. I thought it would be fantastic to go. I was really interested to know what had happened to these places after the end of the Soviet Union and at a sufficiently long time afterwards that things had settled down a bit. I had actually been to Kazakhstan once before, to the Kazakh Republic, but on a train travelling from Uzbekistan — from Bukhara — to Moscow, which is an eighty-five hour journey, which was unbearable. We travelled 'hard-class'. We had a crooked, very Soviet, Gogolian character, called Mikhail Mikhailovich who organised our trips. He was a very large and portly Soviet crook who flew back to Moscow and put us on the train. We were on the train along with chickens and army recruits returning after their military service, and that wasn't a good time to be in the army. For two days, pretty much, we went through the Kazakh steppes and all you could see was a camel every few hundred yards. We did not see the Aral Sea because there wasn't any Aral Sea — there should have been but it had dried up. I was fascinated and haunted by this land.

So, that was what got me to Kazakhstan first of all. But when I was planning to go there, I felt quite uneasy as well because I really did not know Kazakhstan and there was a pressure to make some work and I felt that it was quite superficial to transplant myself and make something about Kazakhstan and about the Soviet period, or post-Soviet period. What I ended up doing was really thinking about what it meant to be travelling to Central Asia and I read lots of travelogues from the 18th and 19th centuries, earlier even, of Central Asia and about the Great Game. I also read an article on a website about eagle hunting in Kazakhstan and I managed to find a museum of eagle hunting[2]. I went and visited this museum and made a film about making a film about the eagle hunters. That was what took me there. That landscape is the Charyn canyon, which is on the postcards that are in the exhibition. It is

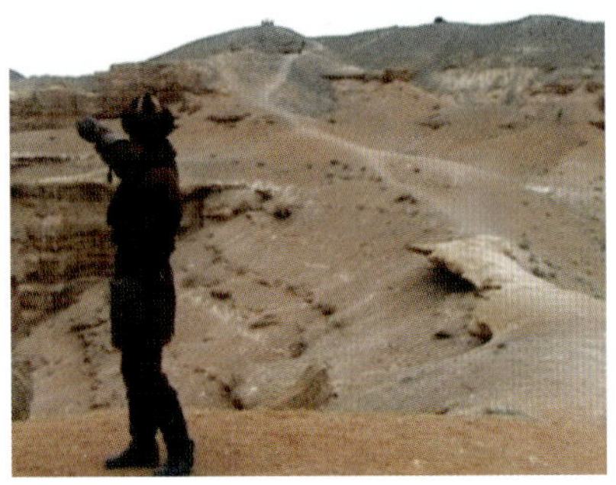

called the Valley of Castles. That was what triggered, in part, the beginning of this project. I had this kind of strange sense of instant recognition — not even strange, because recognition is not strange. There was a familiarity with this landscape that should have been completely exotic, but it wasn't exotic because I'd seen it in Westerns.

OH: One of the things that struck me about the desert in *Anarcadia* is that Wild West quality to it. Immediately, and especially when you see the lone figures in it, you imagine the Ennio Morricone music over the top — it is all very 'Man with No Name'. The Soviet equivalents of Westerns had often been filmed in Central Asia because it had this ready-made John Ford landscape. So almost as soon as they went there it was mediated. They went there seeing Westerns. The obsession with America in the Soviet Union, especially in the 1920s, meant that they probably knew that landscape better than they knew Central Asia — people of western Russia particularly. As soon as they went there, that is what they saw. That idea of frontiers seems to link the two countries. When Khrushchev decides in the 1950s that he is going to cultivate the Virgin Lands, which are in Kazakhstan, the city that later became Astana was...

RM: ...it was Tselinograd, which means Virgin Land city. Before that it was Akmolinsk, then it was Tselinograd, then it was Akmola. Then Nazarbayev built Astana on top of it. People seem to have bought the idea that it was built from scratch fourteen years ago, which it wasn't.

OH: I saw a picture in a book of the original city — the city that was built in the 1950s/1960s — looking completely like 1960s Dresden. A block, a big square, another block etc.

RM: The thing about Kazakhstan is that it was a Russian colony — it wasn't called Kazakhstan yet, it was a large chunk of Central Asia. So, the Russians have been in Kazakhstan for quite a long time, but you are right that the huge influx of people there was much later — in the 1960s, and even before the 1960s in the 1930s with collectivisation, when a third of the Kazakh population died in forced famine. Forced collectivisation meant all their animals were taken away or killed if they refused to give them to the farm, and nothing grew. Later in the 1960s, Khrushchev was planting corn

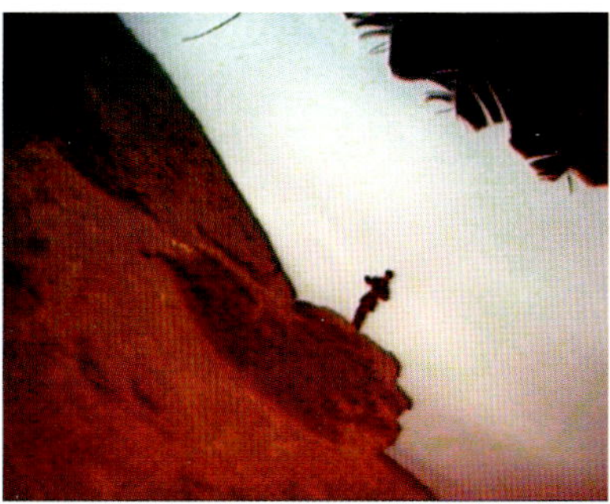

— and we know about the failure of his corn planting... it is not necessarily the most hospitable land for growing in. I think that idea of the Virgin Land is very much like a kind of frontier, that idea that we are going to feed the whole Soviet Union. The archival film in the exhibition is all about linking up Central Asia/Turkmenistan to Siberia — it is like a food route, as well as being about the factories along the way. It is about feeding the whole of the Soviet Union. [...]

RM: Ukraine was the bread basket of the Soviet Union, but with a kind of Russian gloss because of Kievan Rus, so it was supposedly, or historically, part of Russia...

OH: ...and vice versa. With the prospecting and so forth, I kept thinking of Charlie Chaplin's *The Gold Rush*. The idea that you go there and you end up eating your shoe. It is a very bleak version of the gold rush.

RM: Definitely that was an inspiration. I went to this place where the station is because I had heard about a giant railway station that had been built in the desert, a hundred kilometres from Almaty[3]. The first time I heard the story, I was told that it was Khrushchev who was going to build a new capital because he wanted to establish power away from the original existing capital of the republic, Alma-Ata. Then I heard from an architectural historian that this couldn't possibly be true and it must be the Stolypin reforms, before the First World War. I managed to get to this place, which was a village, confusingly called 'Kazakhstan'. Three houses, two of them were uninhabited — now two of them are inhabited. When I went there first it was September and it was completely dry and very desert-like. It was much more lush in the film because they had a late spring. I got there only to find that two weeks before the station had been destroyed and the brick had been salvaged[4]. So I was really rather disappointed because I'd had this idea that I was going to make a film in this station in the middle of the desert and there was no station — although there were still the remains of the station. I came away and something kept niggling — this sense that I did not know what the history of this was. I could not find out what had actually happened: why this place was built, what it was for; why there was this huge station in the middle of the desert but no tracks had ever been laid. I heard another theory when I was in the archive in Almaty where I got the

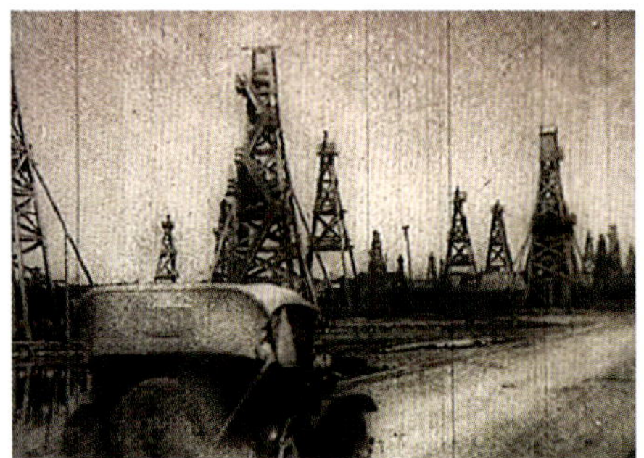

photographs and the film, from a filmmaker who said that because Almaty is on a fault-line and it was completely destroyed by an earthquake in 1909, that they were building a capital station away from Almaty just in case the city was destroyed again by an earthquake. Now this seems a little implausible, and also rather a stupid thing to do because it really is in the middle of the desert — it would make a hopeless capital. But they did make a new capital in the middle of the desert, so maybe it is not a hopeless idea — I am not going to predict!

OH: One of the things that I found interesting in *Anarcadia* was the way the two characters — and it seems quite pointed — see something completely different. One of them sees this wilderness and idealises it — idealises the fact that he cannot see history and he cannot see time. These things are just obliterated. But for the woman, the archaeologist, when she is walking around, every single bit is infused with an enormous amount of history and a complex temporality. Is a comment intended there on the soul's persisting tendency to try and look for wildernesses, to try and find somewhere that is untouched by man? Yet when you actually get there you would have to have fairly skewed eyes to not see that touch — there are power lines everywhere. There is an electrical hum that runs through the soundtrack. It is a myth that this could ever be a wilderness.

RM: I think those things are happening. It is also very much about their professional gaze. They are both equally alienated — neither of them is of the place. Even though she is Kazakh, she is not of that place — she cannot be — there is a desire to be in a place. He postures for himself, as a cowboy does. He sees himself as a pioneer — the idea that he is the first person to ever see 'this buried cube of world'. In fact that is a quote, pretty much, from an oil prospector that I met before I went out there, which I did to make the character more real. One of the things that this geologist said to me — he had worked in other deserts, not Kazakhstan, but in Algeria for BP — was that he did have this sense of being a pioneer. You are seeing something that no one else has ever seen before. It might be due to the BP accident in the Gulf of Mexico, but he very much had the defensiveness of the pioneer, where it is really important that you do not see what is there, because otherwise you are not able to be a pioneer.

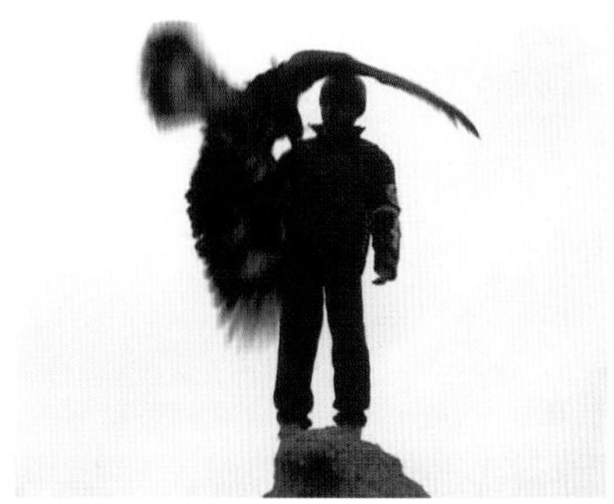

OH: Yes, it always seem to entail, whether in the USA in the 19th century, or even a hundred years later, that you are chancing upon places that already exist and seeing them in a very....

RM: In Azerbaijan where the oil comes out of the ground, all the big oil companies were there at the beginning of the 20th century. One of the things the prospector did say is that they always have the archaeologists in first and that they never drill where there is archaeology. By the time I met him I'd already written the characters. In a way they kind of came out of the landscape. [...]

OH: There is something the archaeologist says at one point — 'I used to live in the future.' That post-Soviet idea seems particularly important there. Although it is quite far from the site, I immediately thought of Baikonur in Kazakhstan, the space city where the Soviet space programme was based and where it was all taking off from. This sense of futurism that the Soviet Union had at various points through its history, whether through its space programme or the idea of building a more equal society, and which disappeared in the 1990s. There is a sense of a temporality that is not there anymore. It seems to link up with earlier on when the prospector is celebrating the fact that there is no time here, but she seems to see that more as a loss.

RM: It is very important. Baikonur was important wherever you were in the Soviet Union. Space is the only innocent future in a way. It is connected with Laika, the dog that was sent into space, and Yuri Gagarin. It is a kind of innocent future. When she is saying, 'I used to live in the future,' there is this idea of potential — that it is always going to be happening but has not happened yet. But if you were given a dacha, then that was great — and a new dacha would have been even better. That whole idea of a dacha transplanted to Kazakhstan is ridiculous, because the landscape is not right for it. A dacha is a wooden hut in the forest outside of Moscow. It is a Russian thing, not a Central Asian thing. It is not a yurt, so a concrete yurt does not work. There is also an idea about the potential being replaced by an imaginary future that is then replaced by another imaginary future, and yet you somehow never have the power to realise it or say what it is. It is like a future or a dream that is imposed upon you, the idea that you do want this and this is what it is. The Zen gardens of millionaires came out of a

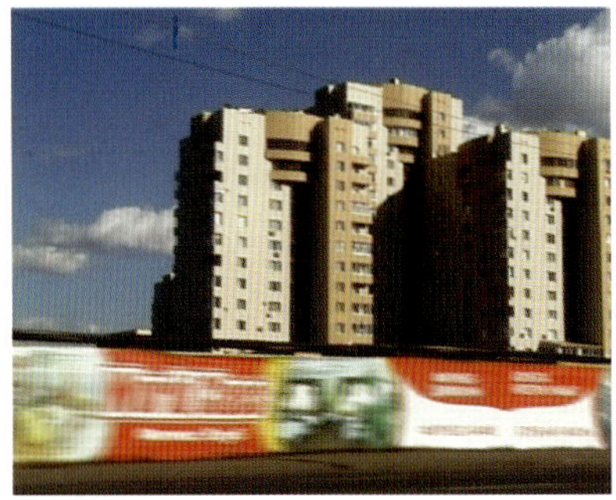

completely chance meeting in St James's Park with a Kazakh stonemason who made Zen gardens for wealthy Kazakhs in Almaty.

OH: The idea of this wilderness being created by the water being stolen for someone's Zen garden brings us to *Capital* and to the depiction of Astana. You talk about how the fountains in public places are designed to deter any revolutionaries or protest, or any real public use of the space. While that is true enough, there is something in the way that the letters have this repetition of prince that meant I kept thinking of St Petersburg, which struck me as the Astana of the 18th century. Built in an incredibly inhospitable place, it was a beautiful classical city built on some marshes in the Arctic. Huge numbers of people died building it. That seems to link to Astana where the climate is so inhospitable and where the ragged flags that are out there are torn because the wind is literally shredding them. But then, of course, St Petersburg is famous for having revolutions. Peter the Great's attempt to create this safe city with its gigantic wide prospects and its huge square for military parades does not really work. Is there a sense that Astana could not work in the same sort of way?

RM: Potentially, yes. The problem is that there are not enough people there — no one wants to go there. One of the reasons I was given for the creation of Astana was because it was further away from China than Almaty, which though true, is absurd. Everyone wanted Almaty to be the capital because it already was and because it has a much better climate with three hundred days of sunshine. Everything grows there and it is right next to the mountains — it is beautiful. It has that Stalinist classicism that is attractive. That was one reason — to be far away from China. Although another later story I was told when I was there this time, although I do not know if it is true, is that Kazakhstan is leasing huge swathes of itself to China for agriculture because it is next door — it is just invasion really. Could there be revolution in Astana? [...]

OH: One thing about Almaty is the fact that when all the industry was moved east during the Great Patriotic War — after defeat after defeat and after they had lost all of the Ukraine, Belarus and Western Russia — that at the same time all of the artists and filmmakers were shipped out to Almaty. There is a chapter in the Polish poet Aleksander Wat's book *My Century*,

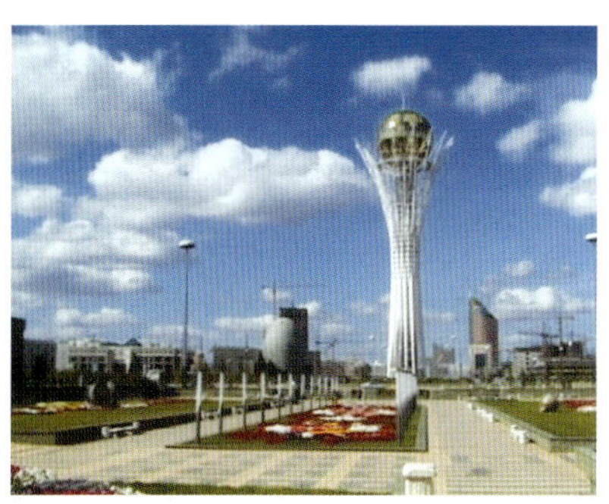

where after Poland was invaded from each side he makes it over to the Russian side and then, being Polish, gets locked up for two years in the Lubyanka[5]. He ends up being let out and allowed to live in Alma-Ata and he thinks he is going to the wilderness, to nowhere. First of all he sees to his surprise that this is a metropolis. He writes about it with this incredible excitement, probably because he has been in prison for two years and anywhere would look good. He writes about it as a metropolis — he is really excited about it as a city and thinks it is wonderful. Straight away he meets Eisenstein, Viktor Shklovsky[6] and Esther Shub[7] — all these people, the cultural elite of the Soviet Union, are all living out in Almaty at that time.

RM: It is true, and they also exiled art that was 'decadent' and which did not appeal to Stalin. So there is an amazing collection of art that is not on display — repressed art. They did not destroy it — they pretty much buried it in vaults in the museum in Almaty[8]. There was a really lively art scene and you were far enough away to survive there. In fact I was talking to a Russian writer about the Russian attitude to Central Asia and he said that Kazakhs are very respected in Moscow. It is the one ethnic minority that is really appreciated somehow. He said the relationship between Russians and Kazakhs is good. Kazakhstan's history is very tied up with Russia. The actress in *Anarcadia* is completely Kazakh and from an establishment family. She is fifth generation Russian speaking. They do not speak Kazakh at all. So the whole nationalist resurgence is very alien to a lot of people and particularly the elite. There is a kind of new elite.

OH: In the footage of Astana there is a sense that it is quite precipitous. You are walking along these shiny blocks and then suddenly you are in this mud track. There is that sense of combined and uneven development. The idea that the temporality there is difficult to figure out is something that seems to run through it. Looking at Astana, and similarly post-Soviet Moscow or Kiev or the newer bits of St Petersburg, what strikes me is how Soviet it is. Not in the sense of socialist but Soviet in terms of imagery. You constantly see this Stalin style skyscraper in the background of Astana — a Seven Sisters style, neo-gothic tower. The monuments seem vaguely expressionist or figuratively kitsch, as if they could have been built in 1951.

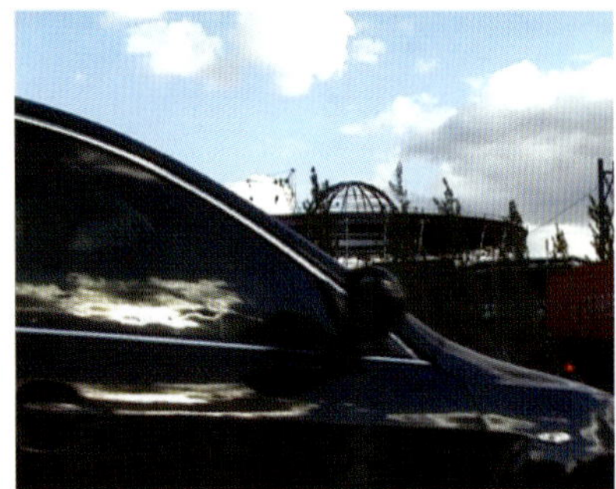 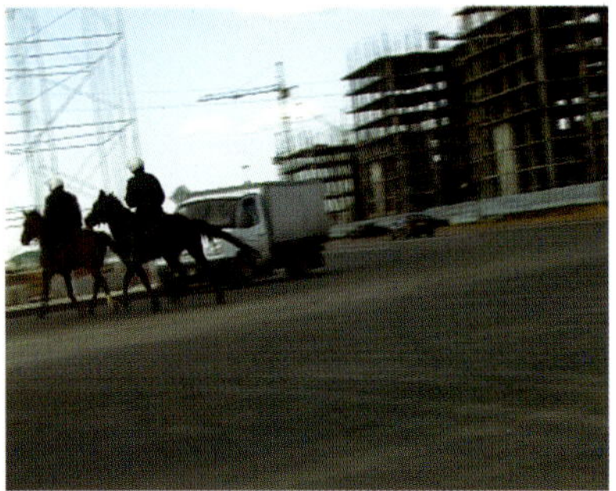

RM: Like Stalinist postmodern.

OH: Yes, because Stalinist architecture is already postmodern. It is already using modernist construction techniques — lots of glass and concrete in order to build bizarre, partly classical, partly Baroque, partly Gothic, partly orthodox kind of skyscrapers. It is already postmodern. After a modernist interregnum of the 1960s, 70s and 80s, they have gone straight back to that. [...]

RM: I was talking to an architect who visited Kazakhstan, going round this and that. She said she had visited the Norman Foster building and that she did not think they finished it — in the sense that it wasn't built by them — because it really does not have the finish you would expect from a Foster building. I had not got so close to know that and the buildings were not finished when I was there. There is a huge amount of money being thrown at it and there is nothing to stop it. There is no resistance to anything. There is not much civil society and not much awareness. There were people who wanted to preserve the Constructivist buildings in Almaty. The architectural historian I met had written a book about the architecture of Almaty and Alma-Ata, and another about the architecture of Kazakhstan and 20th century architecture. So there is an awareness of what was there. But there is no desire within the government to keep anything. There is this horrendous fake history element going on, which I bring up a lot in *Capital*. It is particularly tied up with nationalism, noticeably so in Kazakhstan because it is so far away now from its nomadic roots. The idea of talking about pre-Islamic worship and looking at those Gods and so on, and talking about them as if they matter to anyone is absurd, yet it is happening and it is all tied to the nationalist sentiment.

OH: One of the things that keeps coming to mind is the idea that they have kept everything from the Soviet Union except the egalitarianism and the internationalism. Everything else, the power structures, the architecture, the sense of dominance and the pressure, all seems to be there but without the actual Socialist element, which is quite discredited. Everything else is there. [...]

OH: Rowan Moore wrote an article in *The Observer* quite recently[9] and had this quite wide-eyed approach. He says that previously you can find some utopian potential in these various capitalist dreams and draw it out — like the Russian radicals of the 19th century obsessed with Crystal Palace, for instance. This

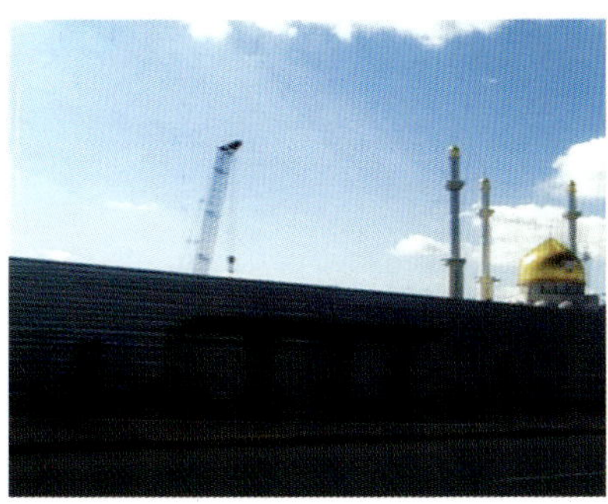

totally capitalist thing but they loved it and wrote about its potential. So, is there anything in somewhere like Astana where you can say that there is an idea here or there is something here that could be salvaged, or is it just horrible?

RM: I do not think you can salvage it as an idea. What is interesting is that things can be salvaged because of detail. There are details that are important, that contradict the overall picture. Both the films and the work are coming out of detail because the overall picture that you get, or that you are given, or that you see, is banal or it is too generalised. Even talking about the post-Soviet landscape as something general is very problematic because each place has a different history. Much of it is often suppressed, now as well as then, because people want to forget and do not want to talk about trauma because it is trauma. I met an architect doing very much his own thing, producing these complex four or five dimensional designs, a Buckminster Fuller of the Steppes. They are really amazing and very interesting — they should travel and be seen.

OH: But are for the drawer, as they used to say.

RM: Yes, for the drawer — paper architecture. I think there are things like that, that are, in a sense utopian. There is a difference and friction between a sentimentalising idea of the future and a utopian future. In a way it is a difference between some of the Constructivists, say Ginzburg, and a futuristic, sentimental, post-Constructivist, Stalinist architecture where it is just completely sentimental. I would say that what is happening here is more of that kind of sentimental, totalitarian architecture, which is not about freedoms at all — it is only freedom in the sense of not asking any questions so that you cannot be contradicted. It is an obedient sort of freedom.

1 On 7th April 1990, a law was passed in the Soviet Union allowing a republic to secede if its residents voted for it in a referendum. This was the beginning of the end of the Soviet Union, with Lithuania declaring independence. After the collapse of the August Coup in 1991, the official end of the USSR came on December 26th 1991, with the dissolution of the Supreme Soviet of the Soviet Union.
2 The BBC correspondent, Ian McWilliam, put me in touch with the museum.
3 The city was called Alma-Ata during the Soviet period, and was subsequently renamed Almaty. However people still sometimes call it Alma-Ata.
4 I was told by the inhabitants that the bricks were sold to a man who built a spa on the Kapchagai reservoir.
5 The Lubyanka is the popular name given to the KGB headquarters and prison, on Lubyanka Square
6 Viktor Shklovsky was one of the founders of the critical theories and techniques of Russian Formalism
7 Esther Shub was a pioneering Soviet filmmaker
8 Kasteev Museum, Almaty
9 http://www.guardian.co.uk/world/2010/aug/08/astana-kazakhstan-space-station-steppes

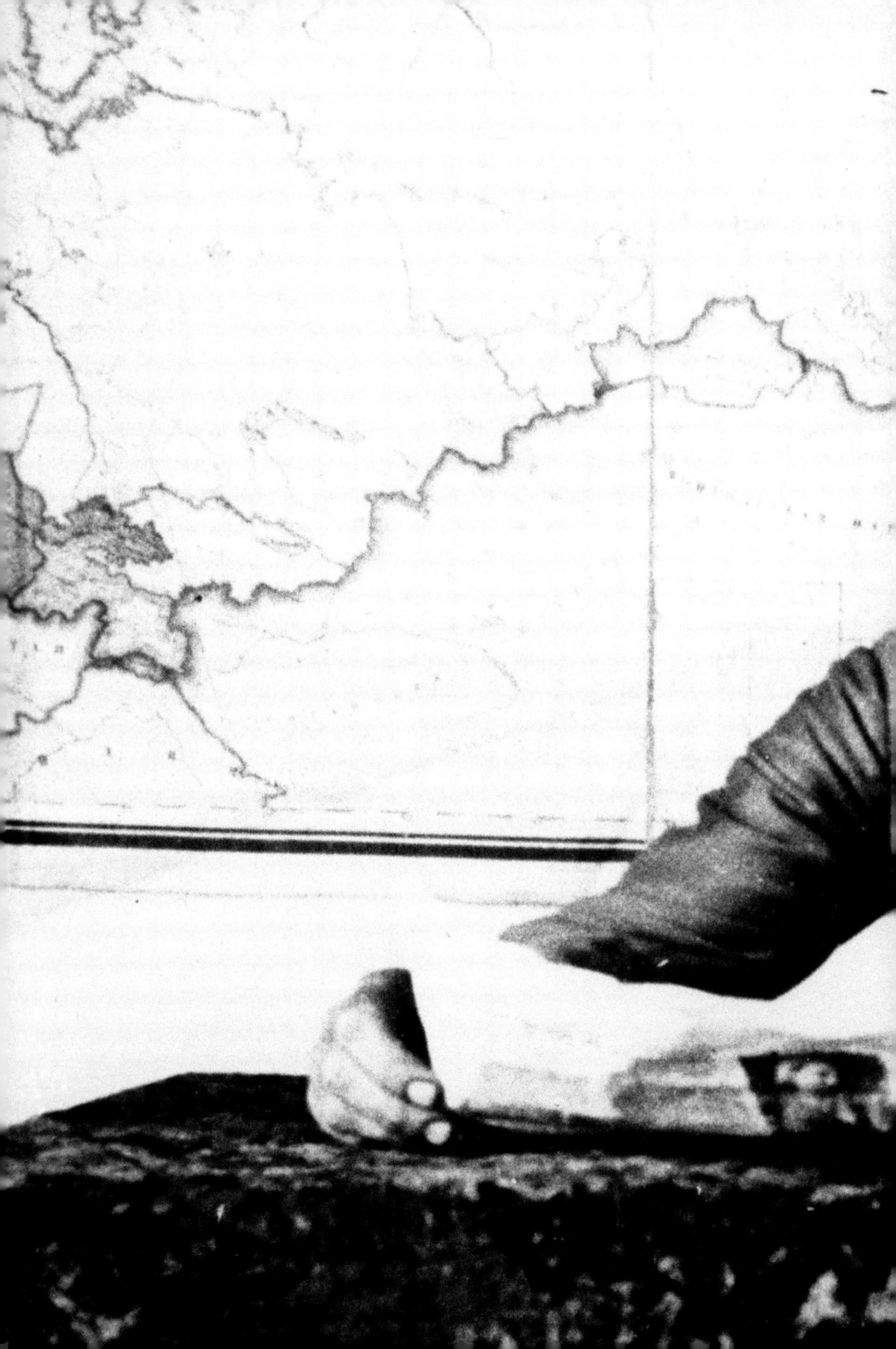

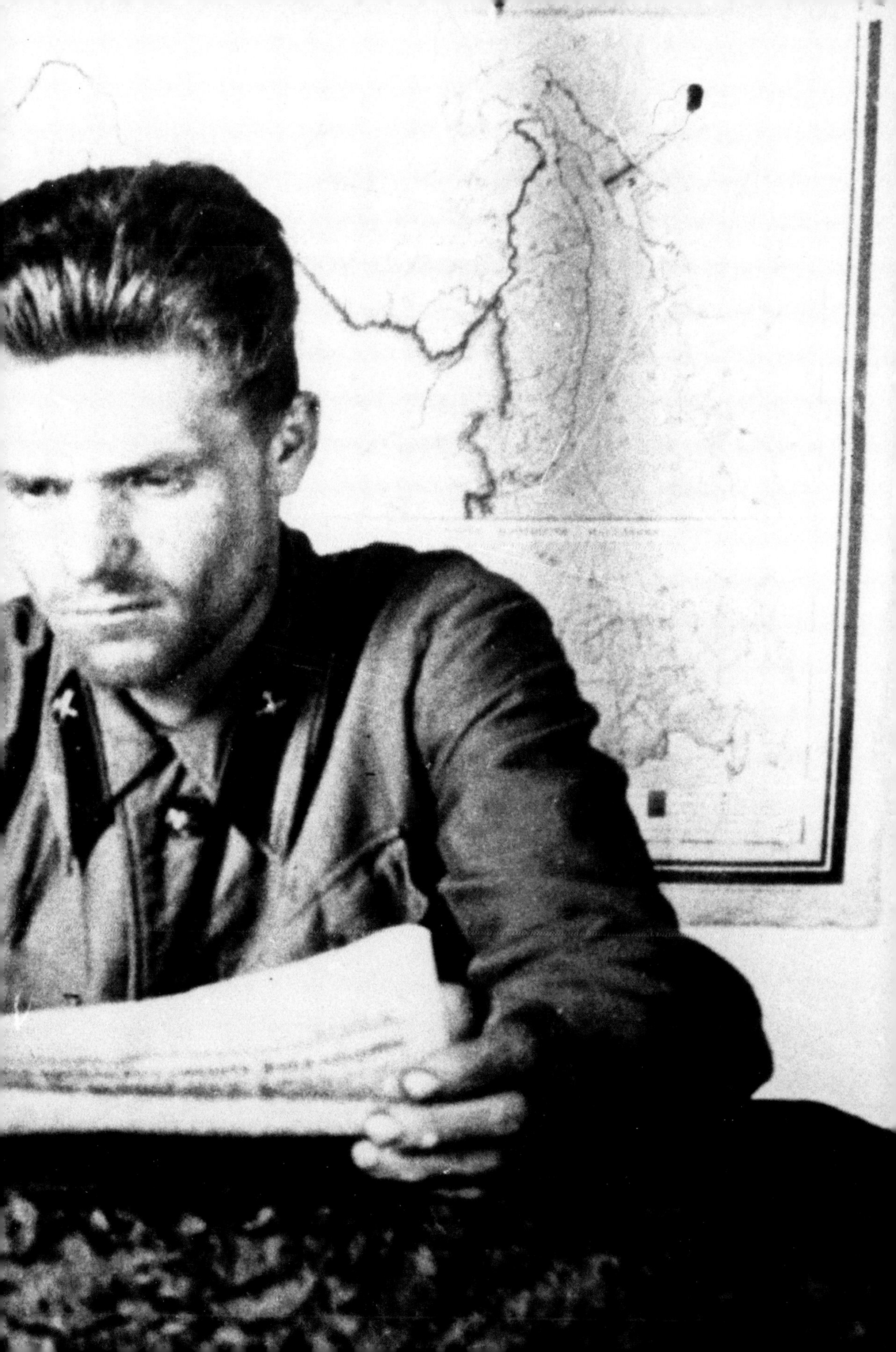

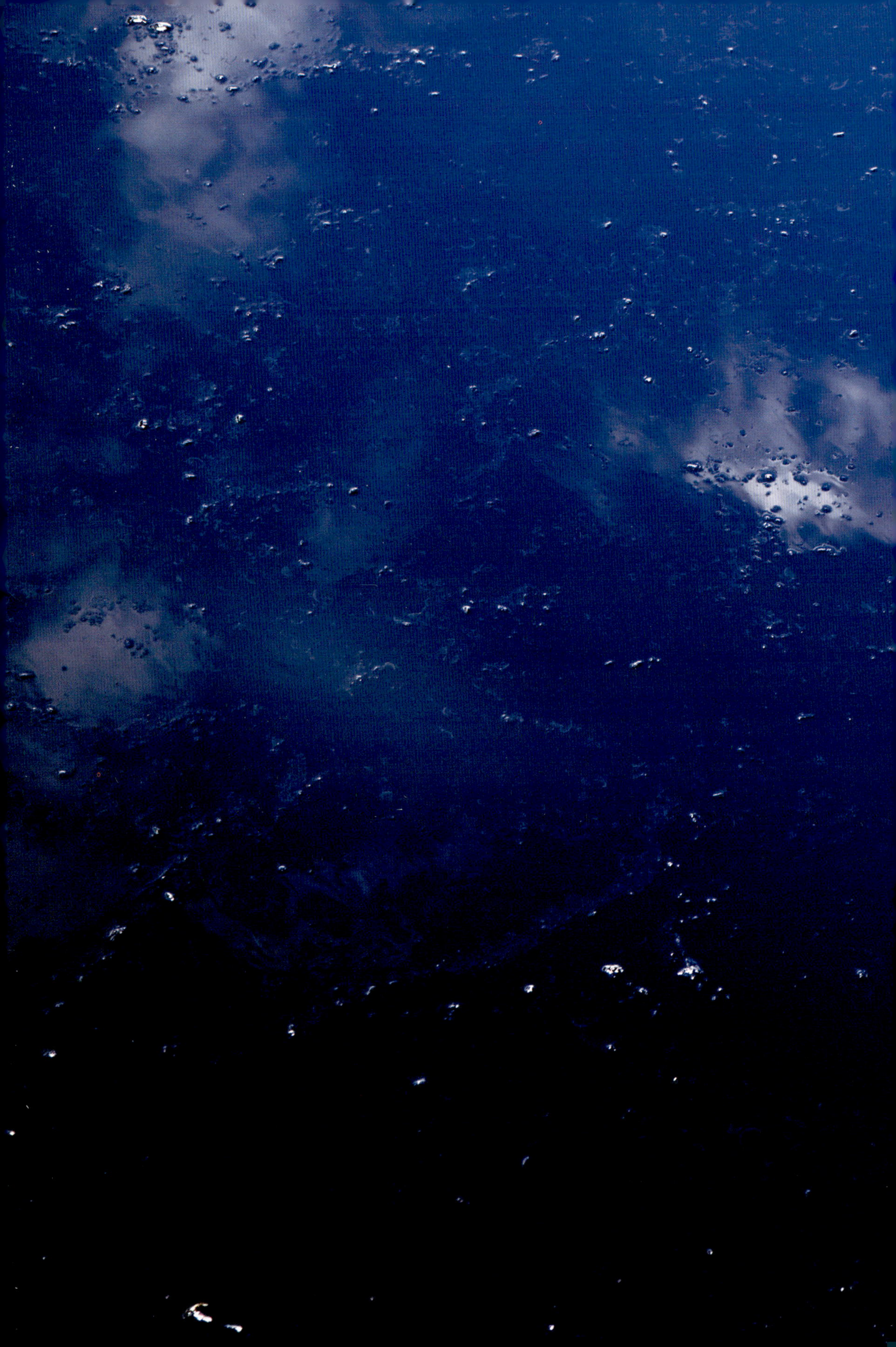

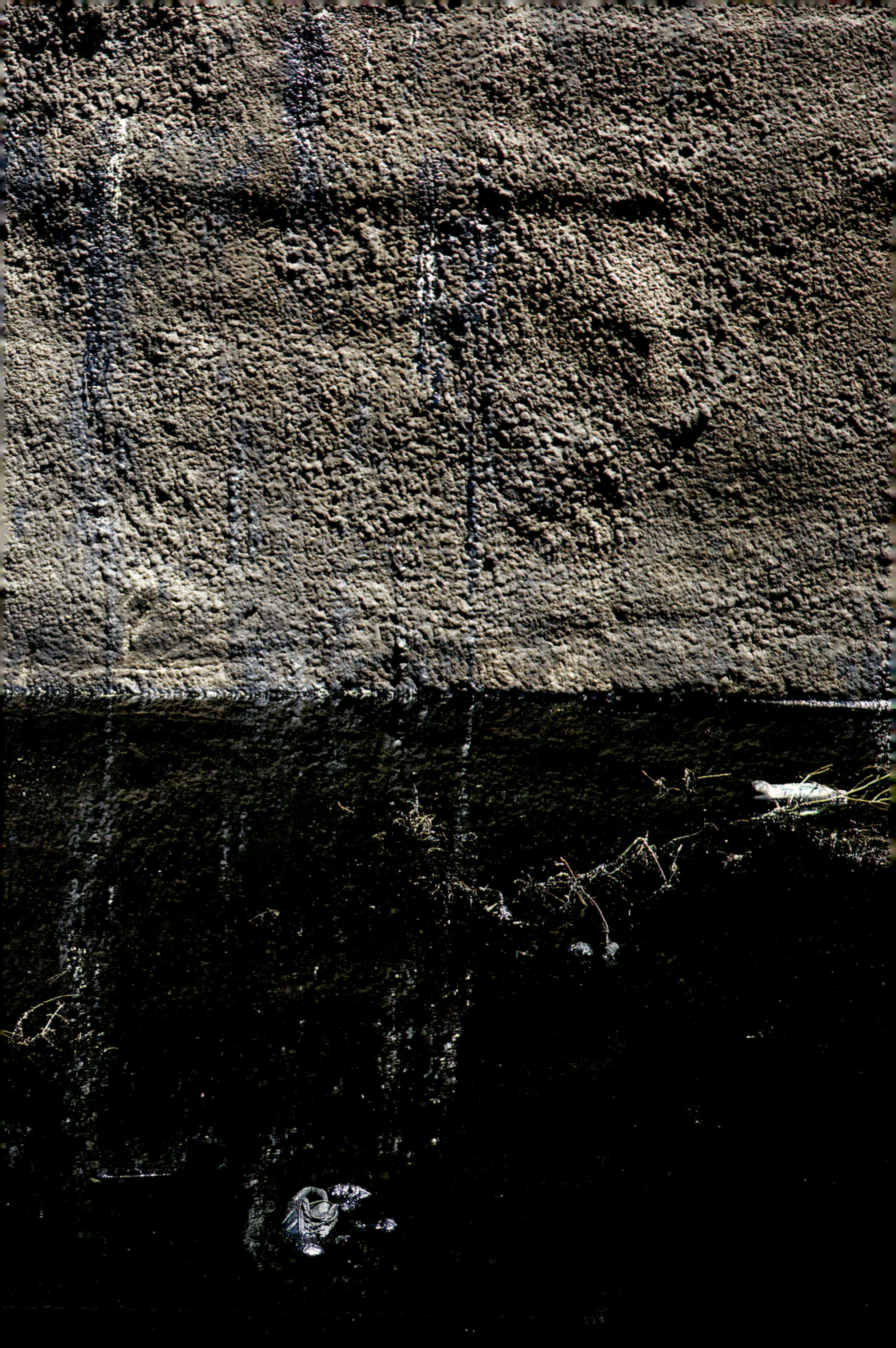

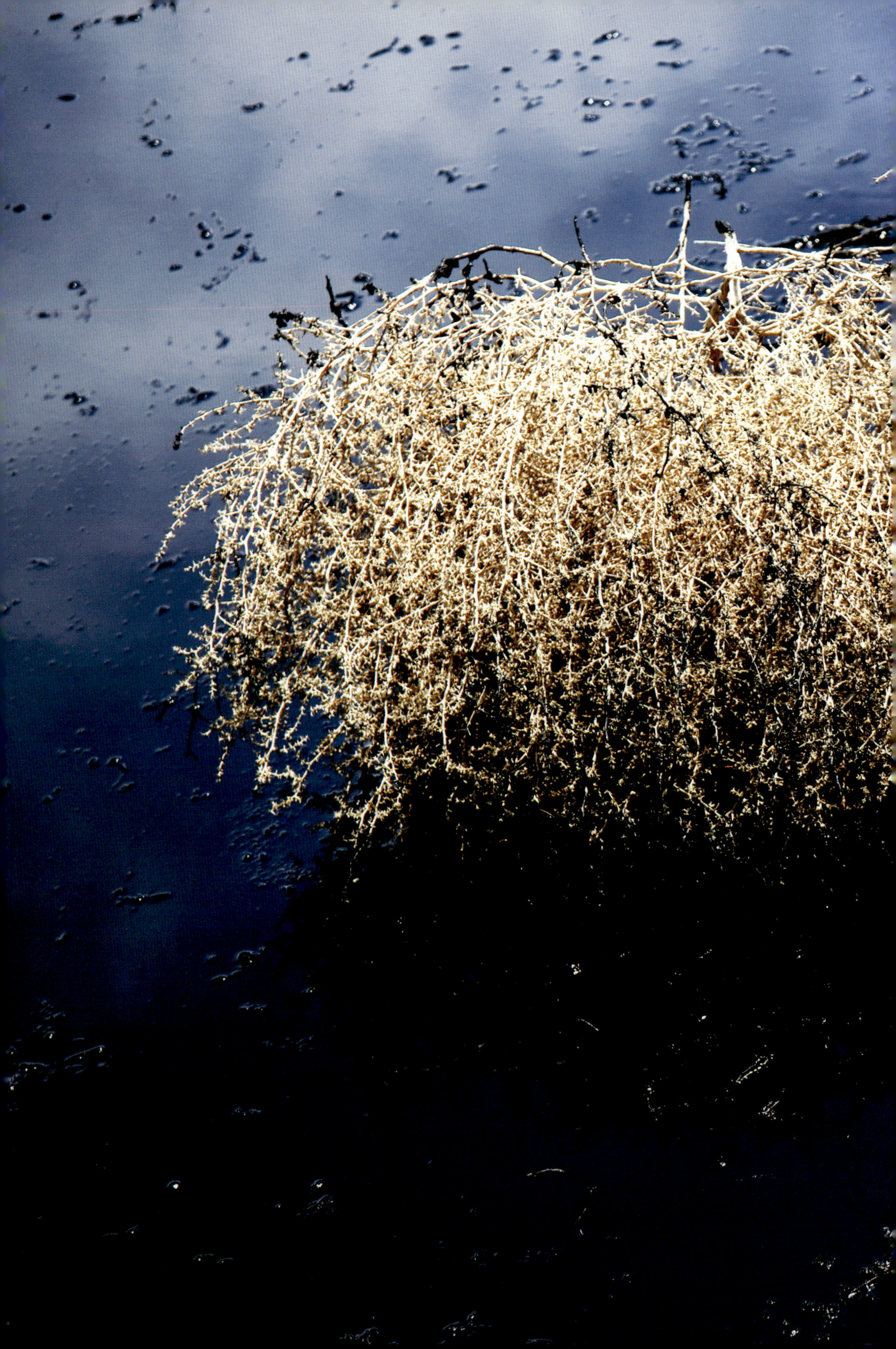

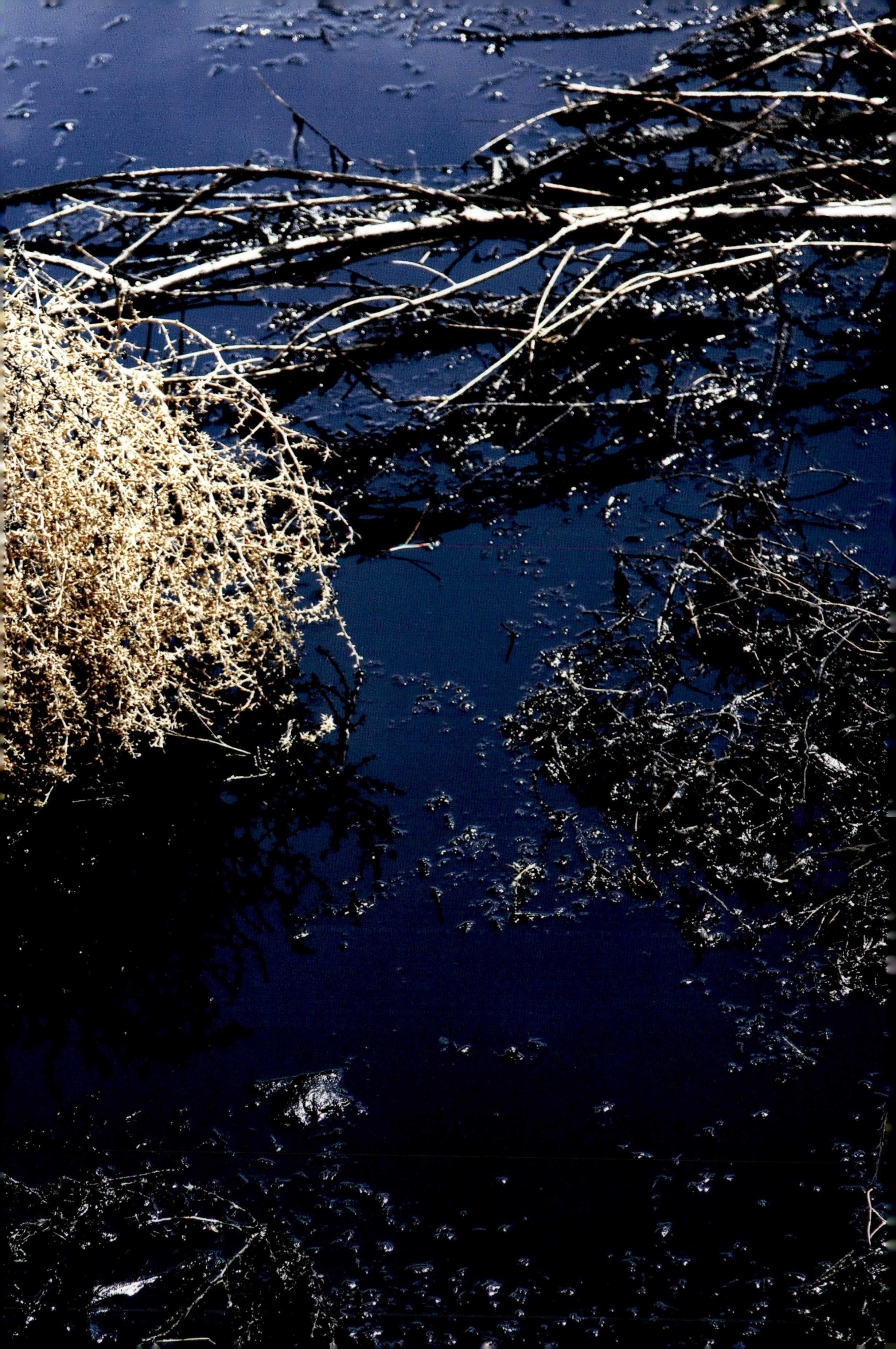

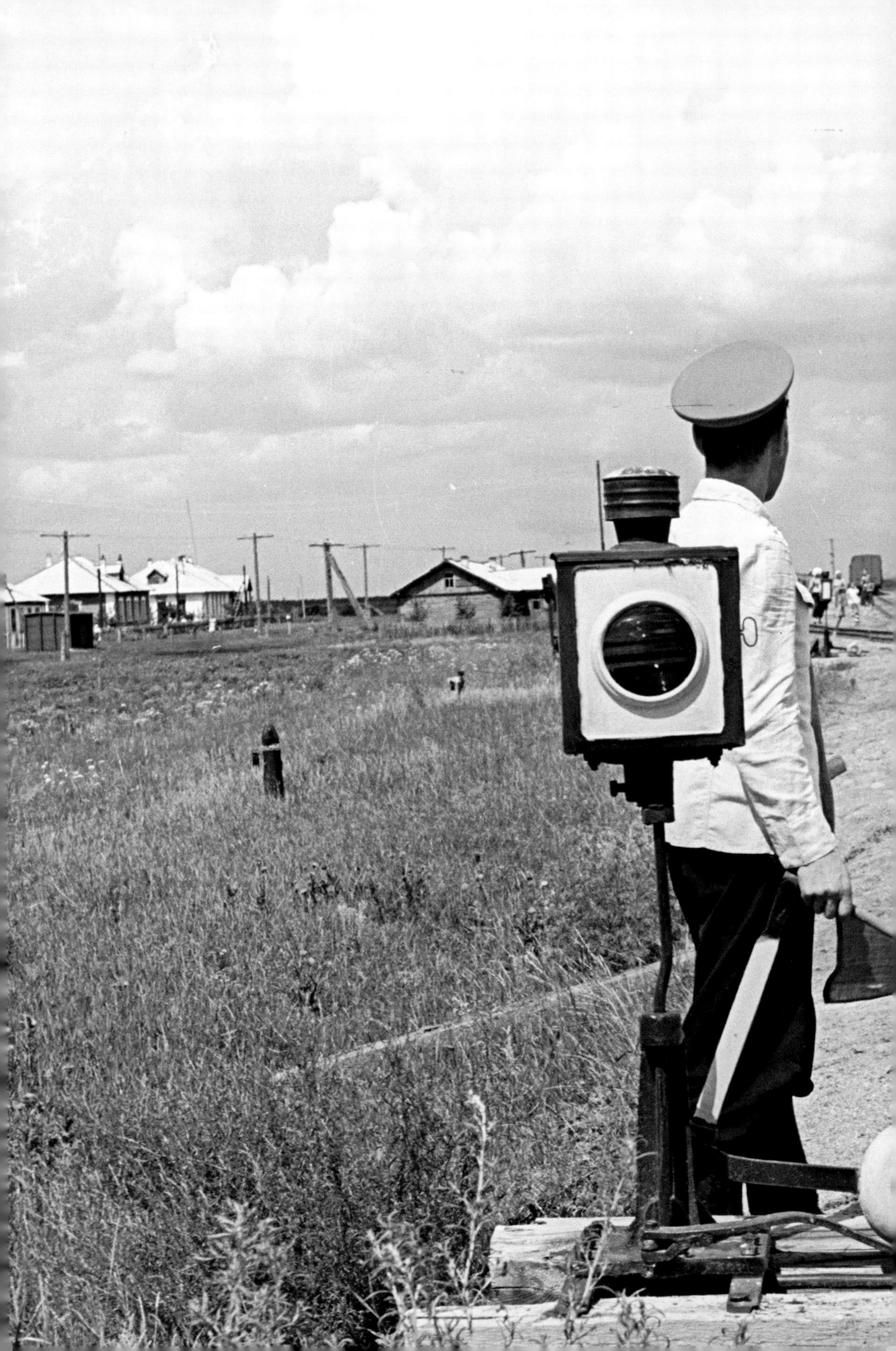

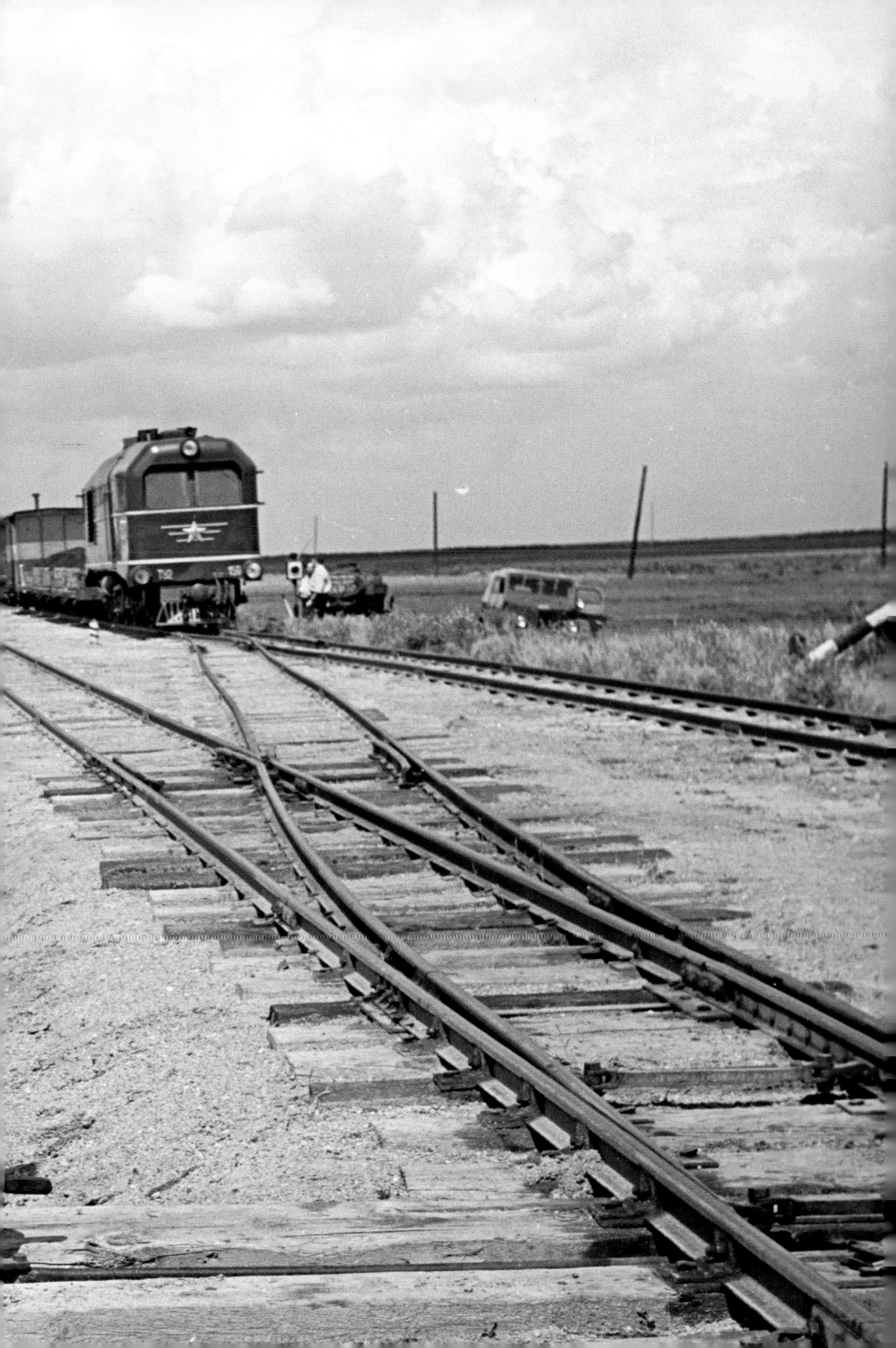

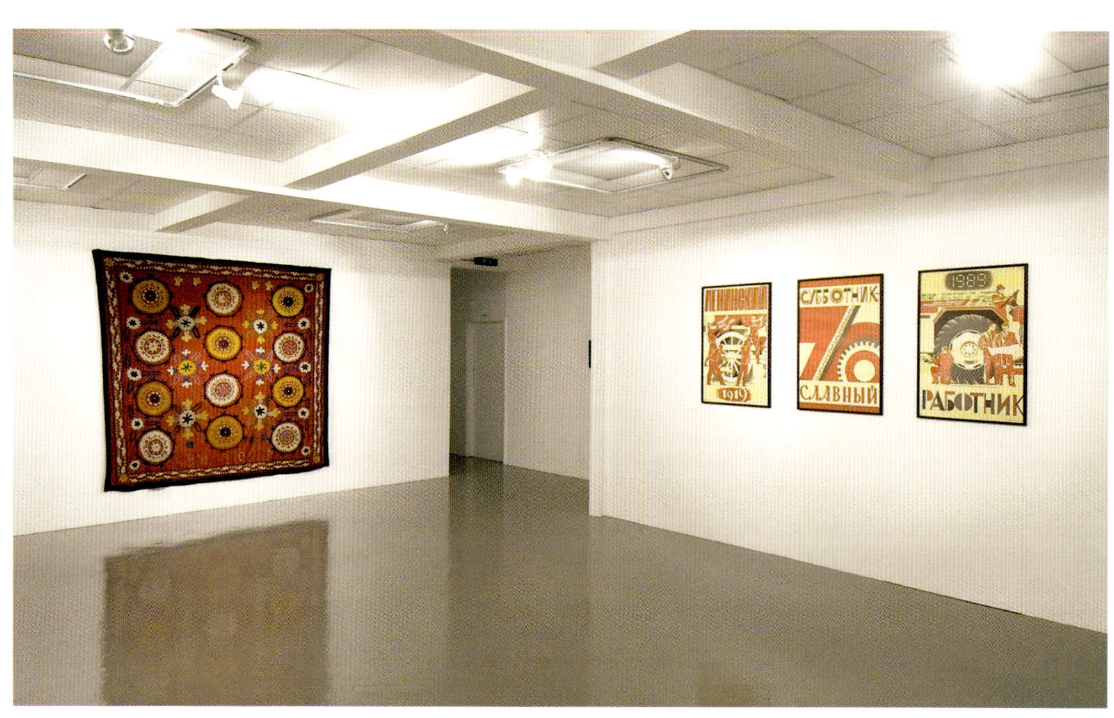

LIST OF WORKS

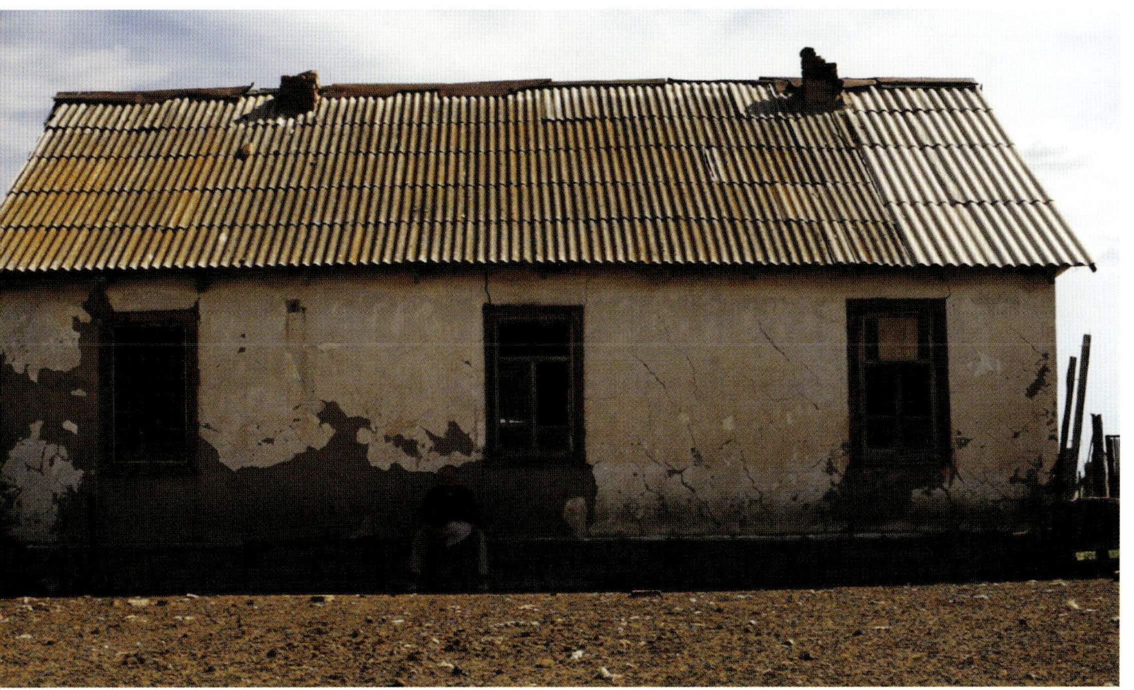

ANARCADIA
High definition video, 35 minutes

Actor	George Drennan
Actor	Saule Suleimenova
Director of Photography	Bevis Bowden
Music composed by	Kuat Shildebayev
Location Sound	Brada Barassi
Sound consultant	Mikhail Karikis
Producer, Kazakhstan	Yuliya Sorokina
Production manager, London	Karen Murray
Archaeology consultant, Kazakhstan	Ruslan Sherbayev

Co-commissioned by Film and Video Umbrella and John Hansard Gallery, Southampton, in association with Stills Gallery, Edinburgh, Ffotogallery, Cardiff and Castlefield Gallery, Manchester. Supported by Arts Council England, the British Council, and Henry Moore Foundation.

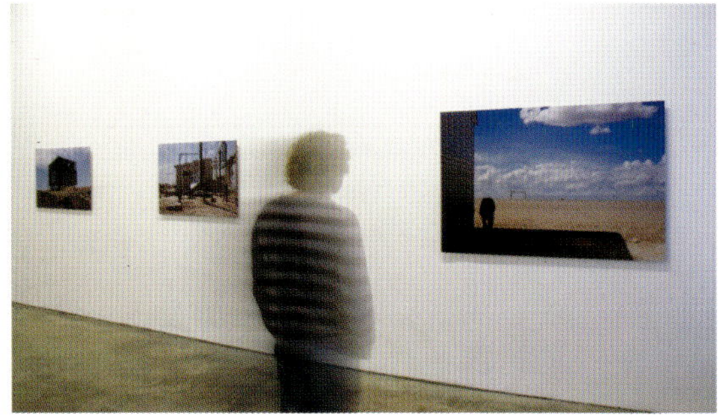 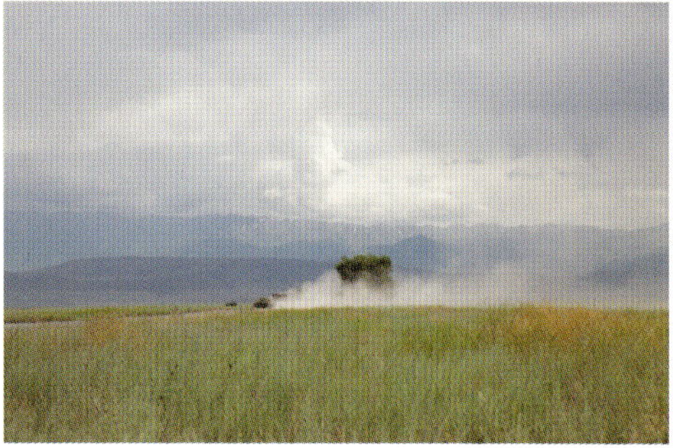

Each exhibition in the initial tour of *Anarcadia* presented the film alongside a selection of photographic and other works expanding the film beyond the frame. These are the *Anarcadia Inventories*.

JOHN HANSARD GALLERY:
Anarcadia Inventory: The Railway Station
The Railway Workers
Ten anonymous photographs from the State Documentary Film and Audio Archive of Kazakhstan, 1939-61, printed on archival paper and framed.
In the yard at the Museum
Photograph, Lambda print on aluminium, 2010
19/XII/1970
Embroidered yurt hanging, Uzbekistan, 1970. Collection of the artist.
'Bringing oil across the desert to the land of the Soviets'
Film fragment, 7-minute loop, from the State Documentary Film and Audio Archive of Kazakhstan, 1930.
Leninskii Subbotnik — Slavnii Rabotnik 1919-1989
Posters, 1989. Collection of the artist.
I was Here Before
Edition of six postcards, 2010
Doesn't belong to anybody
Photograph, Lambda print on aluminium, 2010
Capital
Video, 16 minutes, 2007

STILLS GALLERY:
Anarcadia Inventory: The Back Lot
Desert Mine Desert
Inside Out
Back Lot
Doesn't belong to anybody
Petroglyph
Mirage
Lambda prints on aluminium, sizes variable, 2010-11
I was Here Before
Edition of six postcards, 2010
The Railway Workers
Two anonymous photographs from the State Documentary Film and Audio Archive of Kazakhstan, 1939-61.

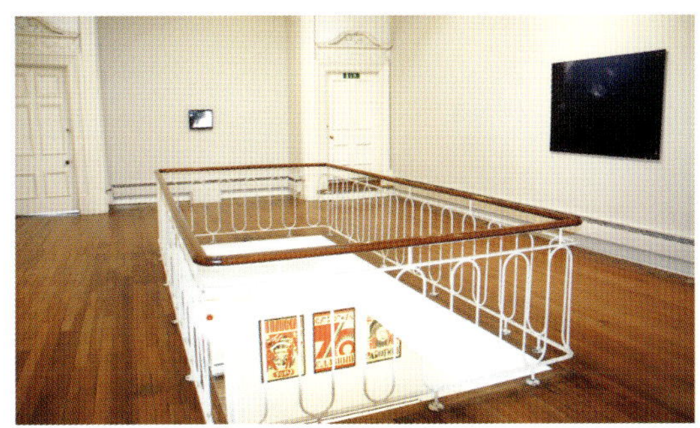

FFOTOGALLERY:

Anarcadia Inventory: After Life

Leninskii Subbotnik — Slavnii Rabotnik 1919-1989

Posters, 1989. Collection of the artist.

I was Here Before

Edition of six postcards, 2010

The Railway Workers

Eight anonymous photographs from the State Documentary Film and Audio Archive of Kazakhstan, 1939-61.

After Life 1 — 4

Four photographs, Lambda prints on aluminium, 2011

'Bringing oil across the desert to the land of the Soviets'

Film fragment, 7-minute loop, from the State Documentary Film and Audio Archive of Kazakhstan, 1930.

CASTLEFIELD GALLERY:
Anarcadia Inventory: The Return

'Bringing oil across the desert to the land of the Soviets'

Archive video fragment, from the State Documentary Film and Audio Archive of Kazakhstan

After Life 1 — 4

Four photographs, Lambda prints on aluminium, 2011

The Railway Workers

Archival photographs, printed on archival paper, from the State Documentary Film and Audio Archive of Kazakhstan

I was Here Before

Edition of six postcards, 2010

Leninskii Subbotnik — Slavnii Rabotnik 1919-1989

Posters, 1989. Collection of the artist.

Desert Mine Desert

2011, Lambda print

Inside Out

2011, Lambda print

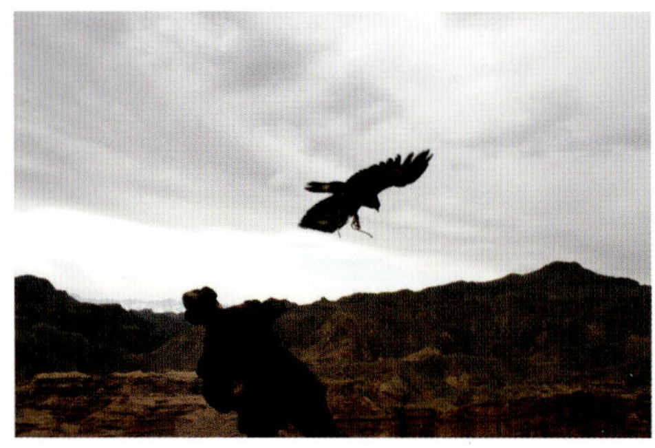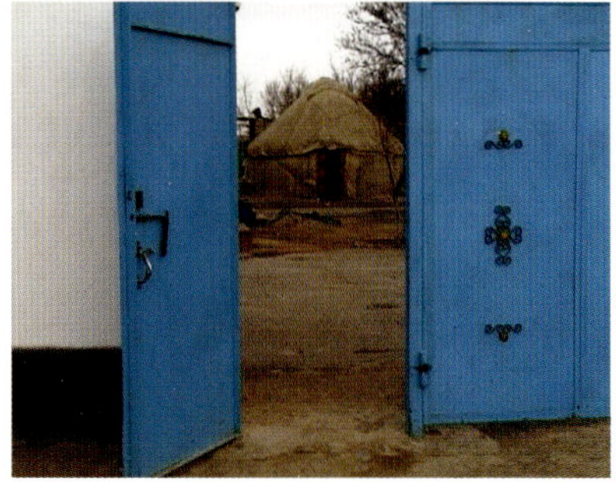

VALLEY OF CASTLES (HUNTING EAGLES)
Single-channel video projection, with sound, 20 minutes, 2007
filmed and edited by Ruth Maclennan, additional filming by Alexander Ugay, Valery Kortun
and Alexei Shindin

Valley of Castles (Hunting Eagles) follows the artist's journey to the village of Nura in
south-eastern Kazakhstan to film traditional Kazakh eagle hunters. The film captures
the hunter's relationship of trust with his bird. At the same time, the idea of an authentic
experience, or authentic view of Kazakh culture, is challenged by the presence of
countless cameras and the Hollywood performance by the handler. There is a suspicion
of a charade being put on for the Western filmmaker, although who is performing for
whom, and who is in control, is open to question. After the journey, against a dramatic
landscape of snow-capped mountains, the film moves into a different register as the
hunter sets the golden eagle free over an empty canyon. The eagle carries a miniature
camera and films its own participation in the ancient Kazakh ritual, dating back to
nomadic times and the practice of 'hunting-magic'. On this hunt the eagle sends back an
image of its own trajectory, and of the world beneath him.

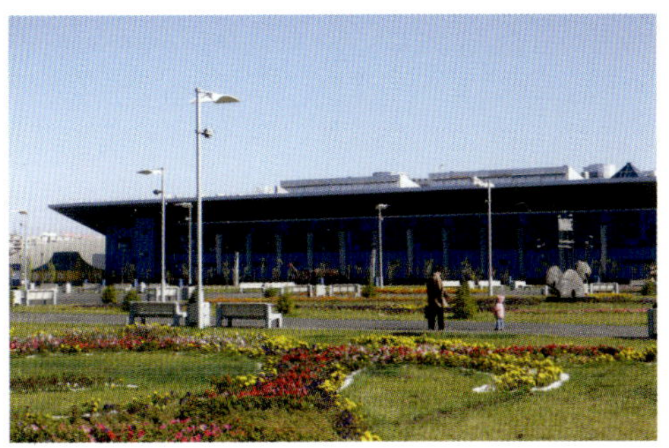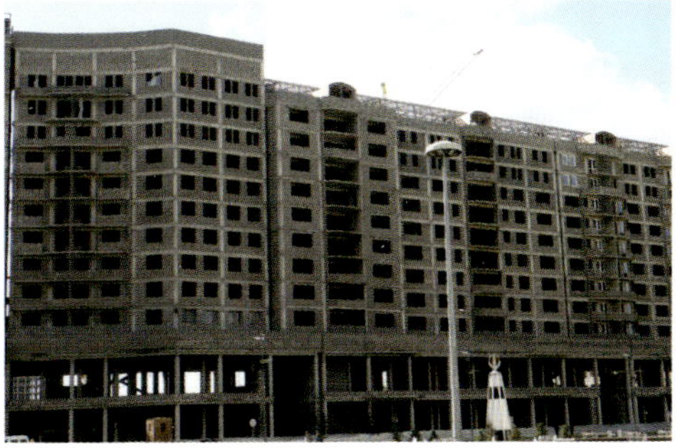

CAPITAL
Video, 16 minutes 50 seconds, 2007

The film echoes past tales of travellers to Central Asia, Italo Calvino's *Invisible Cities,* and even the *Thousand and One Nights* where the story-teller's ability to perform a role and tell a tale is a question of survival. The unnamed city is Astana (meaning 'capital' in Kazakh), Kazakhstan's new capital, built over the existing city of Akmola, which was previously Tselinograd — the centre of Khrushchev's Virgin Lands. The city was founded by President Nursultan Nazarbayev in 1997. *Capital* is dense and fast-moving, the tempo shifting between the slow ungainly steps of an old woman walking down the street and the smooth electronic speed of a glass lift.

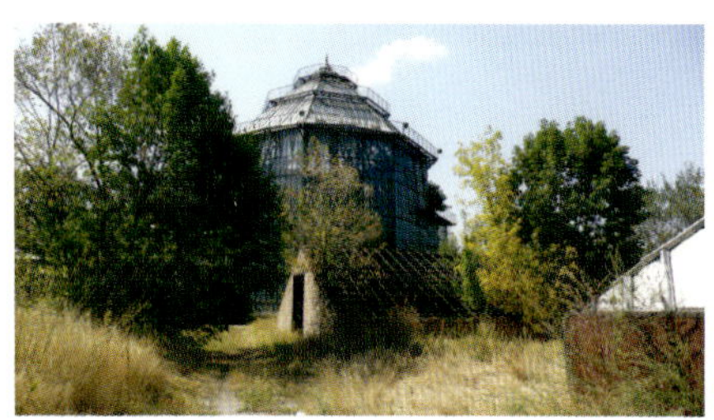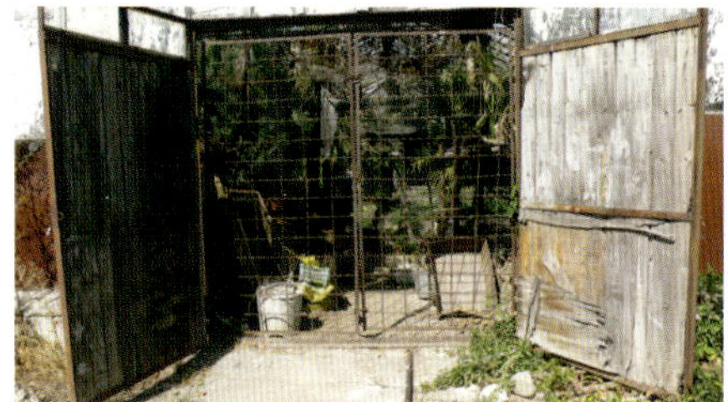

UNTITLED (BOTANICAL GARDENS)
Eight photographs, edition of three, 2007

During the Soviet period, the immense natural resources of Kazakhstan were studied extensively and in many cases exploited almost to extinction. The botanical gardens represent the Soviet vision to categorise and control nature in the service of a political ideal (whether to feed the whole country, or to create new DNA). These dreams are no longer part of Kazakhstan's aspirations, and the gardens and buildings are falling into disrepair. The pictures suggest a settlement that has been abandoned and for whatever reason, left to ruin: a no-place that is alive and growing yet empty of people. The 'zone' from Tarkovsky's film *Stalker* comes to mind. Grids evoke the taxonomies of botany as well as the 'squaring off' used since Renaissance painting. At the same time the pictures point to a utopian desire for an architectural environment that is living, that — like plants and people — ages, disintegrates, and dies.

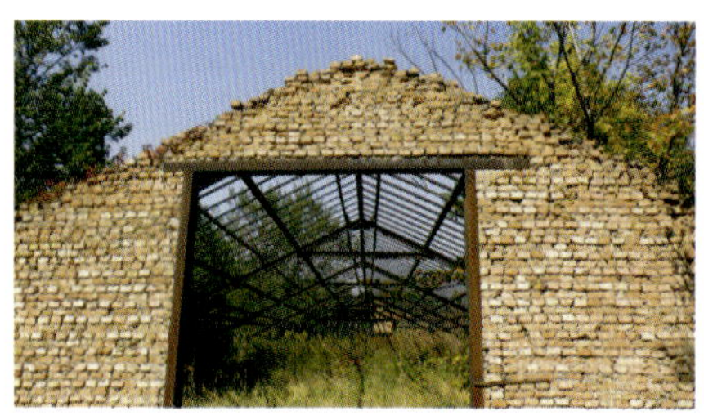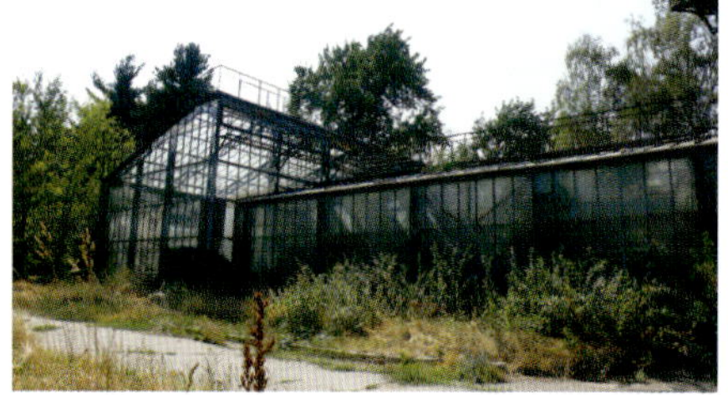

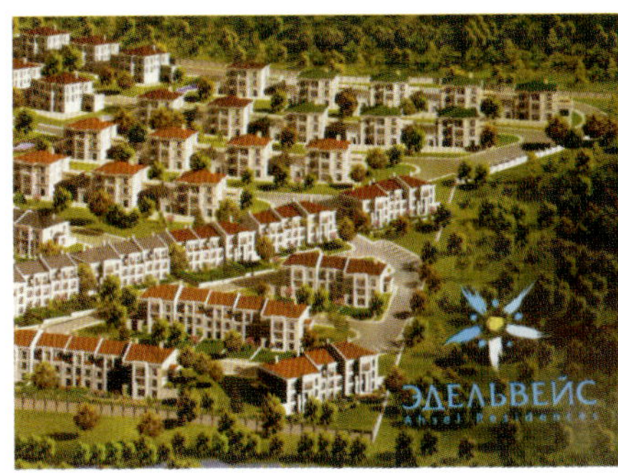

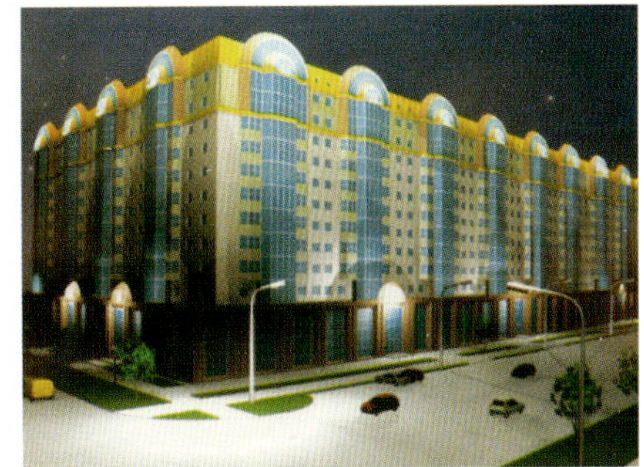

ESTATE

Video slide show, 3-minute loop, 2007

Estate reflects the desire for a perfect life, in a perfect home, in a perfect world. All the worlds depicted are offered up for sale, advertised in magazines, free brochures and on websites in Kazakhstan. The luxury home in Kazakhstan in the 21st century spans a variety of contradictory utopias from Alpine chalet living, to suburban mansion, to Modernist high-rise, and hybrid combinations. Window-shopping for homes is also a favourite British weekend pursuit. The viewer is invited to drift trance-like through a succession of always sunny, rich, glamorous and improbable lives, each vista more seductive than the last.

Capital, *Estate*, *Untitled (Botanical Gardens)*, and *Valley of Castles* were commissioned for the exhibition *Central Asian Project*, at Cornerhouse, Manchester, and at SPACE, London. In addition *Capital* was screened at Zoo Art Fair, London, 2008, and the New York Underground Film Festival (March 2007). *Capital* and *Valley of Castles* toured to Tengri Umai Gallery in Almaty, Kazakhstan, to the Tashkent Biennale of Contemporary Art, Uzbekistan, and to Boom-Boom, Bishkek, Kyrgyzstan, in 2008.

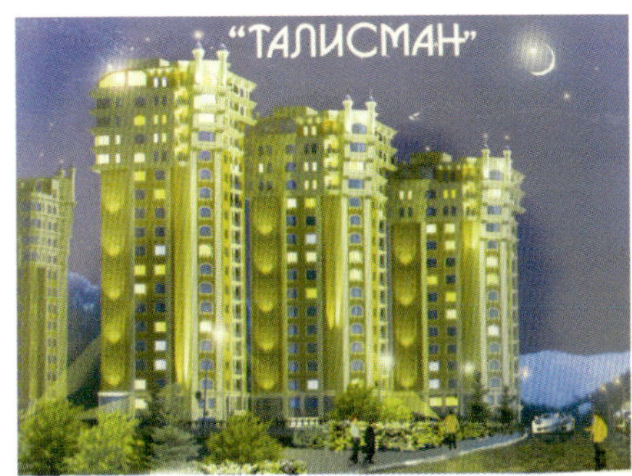

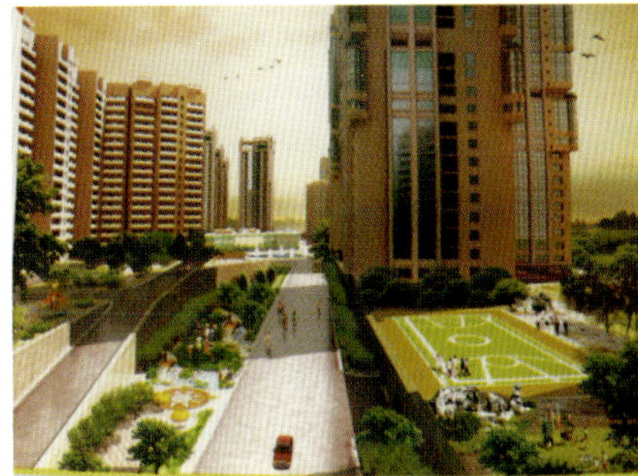

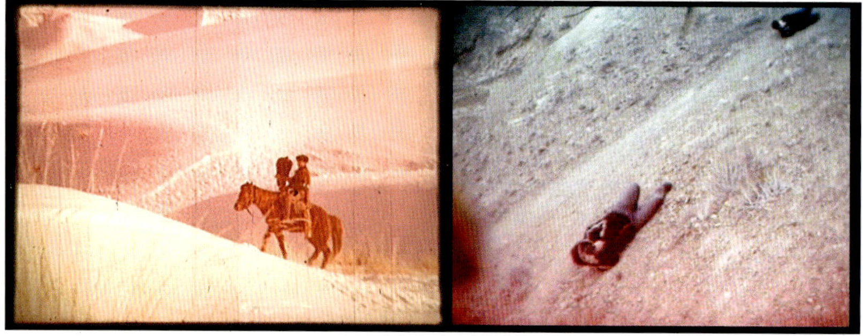

CAPTURE

Two-channel video installation, with sound, 3 minutes 17 seconds, 2007
Includes excerpts from 16mm film 'Berkutchi', 1969, directed by Belyayev, Alma-Ata,
Soviet Socialist Republic of Kazakhstan; and video filmed in Kazakhstan, 2006

Capture juxtaposes footage shot on a miniature camera attached to a Kazakh golden eagle with archive footage of an eagle being captured to be trained for hunting, and then later hunting and killing silver foxes.

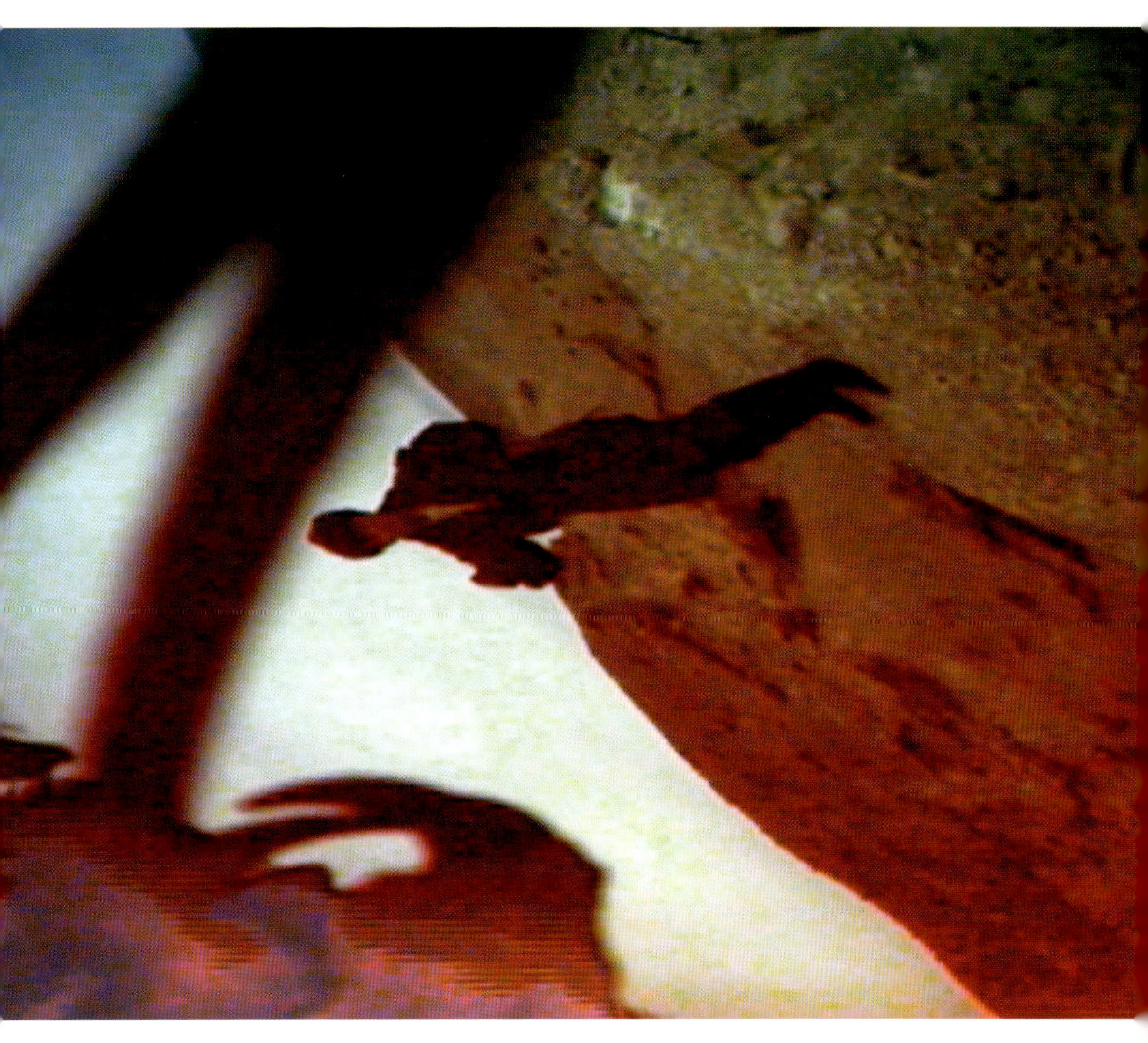

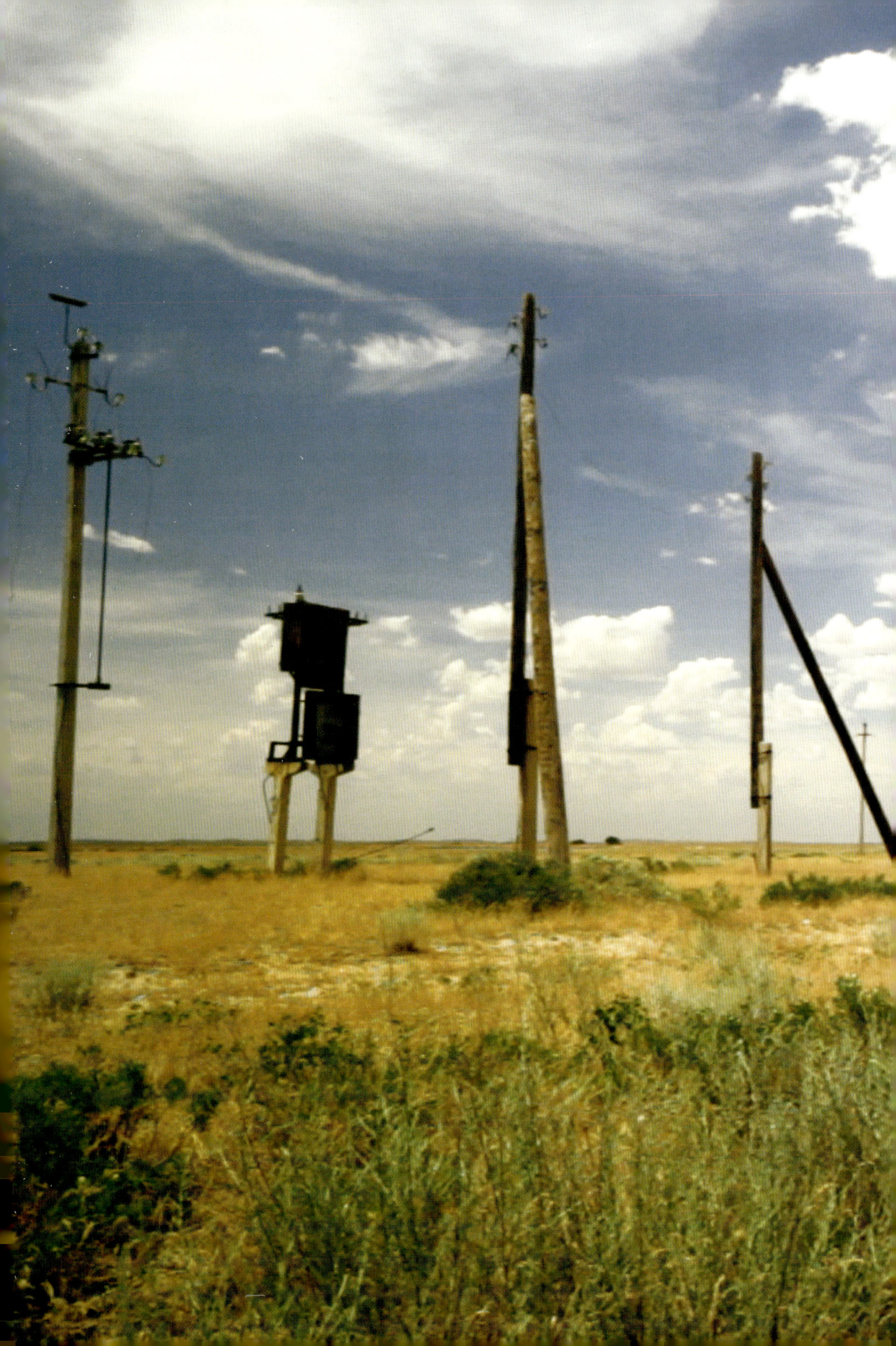

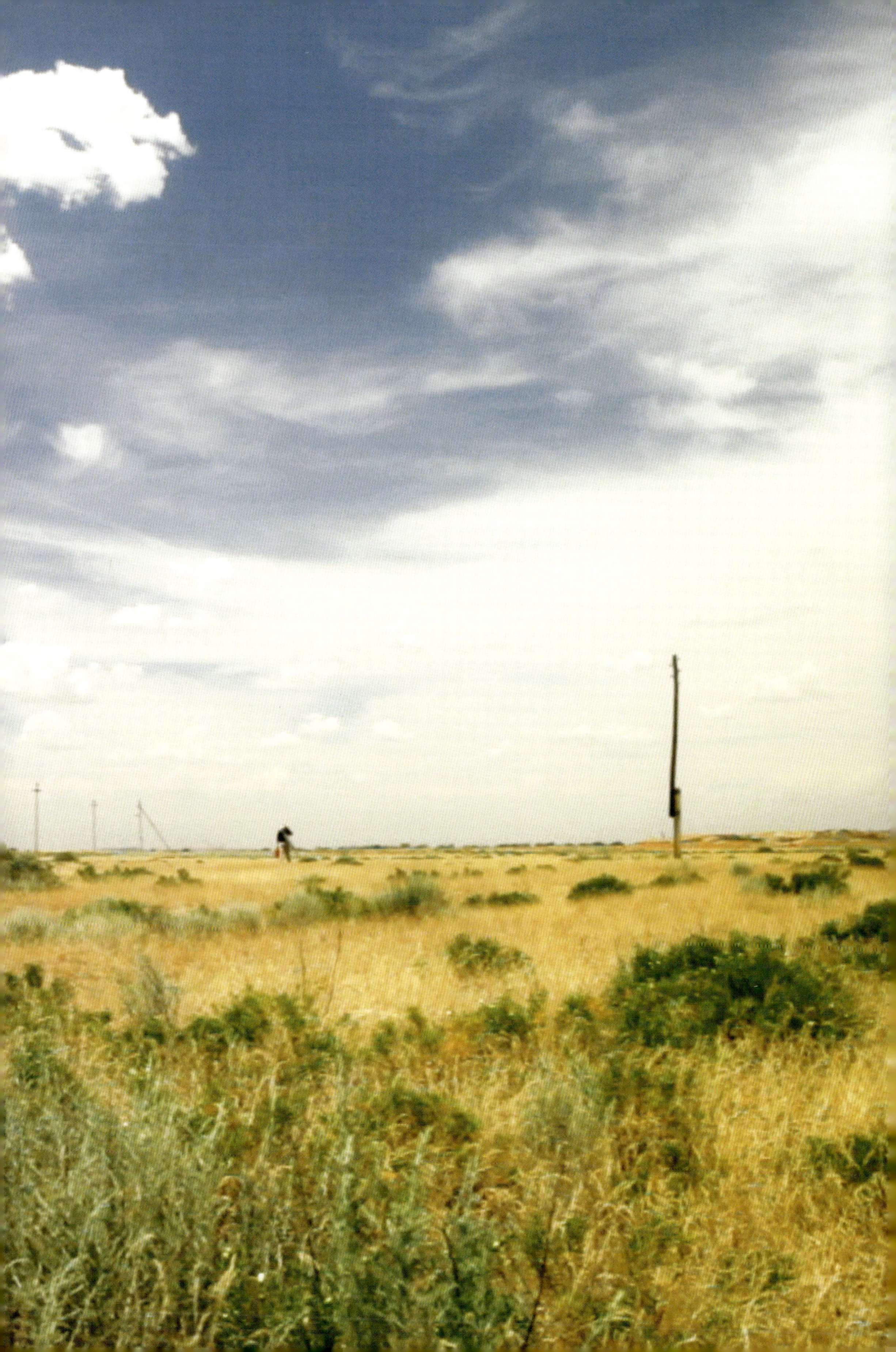

COLOPHON

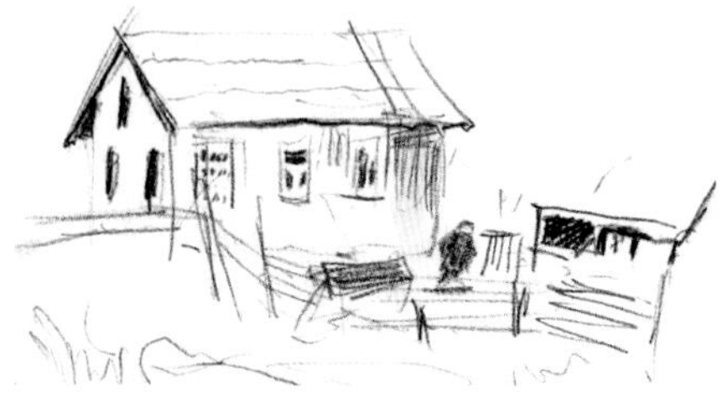

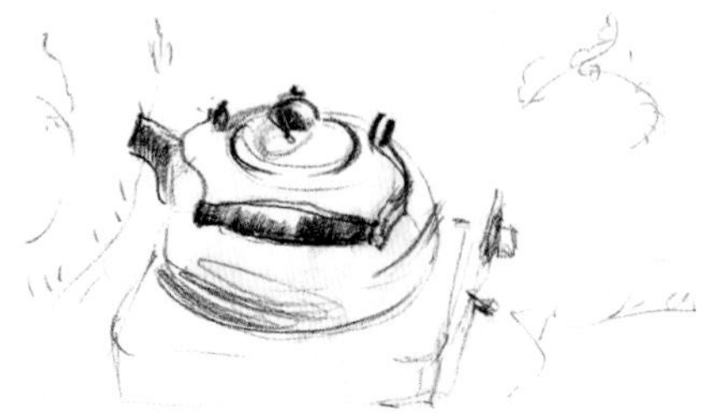

ANARCADIA
RUTH MACLENNAN

Published by Film and Video Umbrella
and John Hansard Gallery

ISBN 978-1-904270-33-1

Edited by Nina Ernst and Steven Bode
With thanks to Honor Beddard
Designed by Secondary Modern
Printed by Calverts
Printed on 170gsm Sovereign Silk;
cover: 315gsm Chromocard

Film and Video Umbrella
8 Vine Yard
London SE1 1QL
Tel: 020 7407 7755
www.fvu.co.uk

LIST OF ILLUSTRATIONS

Cover image: *Doesn't belong to anybody* (detail)
Inside cover: *I was here before* (from the series)
After title page: *Anarcadia* video still
Page 2 and subsequent full-page black and white photographs:
The Railway Workers, anonymous photographs from the State
Documentary Film and Audio Archive of Kazakhstan, 1939-61
reproduced with permission
Page 4: *Anarcadia* installation view, John Hansard Gallery
Page 8: *Anarcadia* video still
Page 11: *Capital* video still
Page 16: *Inside Out*
Pages 17-52: small images throughout the text are video stills
from *Anarcadia* and *Capital*
Page 19: *Petroglyph*
Page 20: *Desert Mine Desert*
Page 23: *Back Lot*
Page 24: *Doesn't belong to anybody*
Page 57: *'Bringing oil across the desert to the land of the Soviets'*,
film fragment, from the State Documentary Film and Audio Archiv
of Kazakhstan, 1930, video still, reproduced with permission
Pages 58-61: *Valley of Castles (Hunting Eagles)*, video stills
Pages 62-65: *Capital*, video stills
Pages 66-75: *After Life* 2,3,1 and 4
Page 78: *Anarcadia Inventory: The Station*, installation view,
John Hansard Gallery
Page 79: *Anarcadia*, video still
Page 80: *Anarcadia Inventory: The Back Lot*, installation view,
Stills Gallery, 2011
Page 81: *Anarcadia Inventory: After Life*, installation view,
Ffotogallery, 2011
Page 82: *Valley of Castles*, video stills
Page 83: *Capital*, production photographs
Page 84: *Untitled (Botanical Gardens)*
Page 85: *Estate*, video stills
Page 86-87: *Capture*, video stills
Page 88-89: *Anarcadia*, video still
Colophon: sketches from location notebook